EVERYONE NEE

Everyone needs a MENTOR

Fostering Talent at Work

David Clutterbuck

with research by
Marion Devine and Helen Beech

Second edition

Institute of Personnel and Development

First Published 1985
Reprinted 1987 and 1990
Second edition 1991
Reprinted 1992, 1993 and 1994

British Library Cataloguing in Publication Data
Clutterbuck, David 1947–
Everyone needs a mentor.
1. Business enterprise. Management
I. Title
658.4

ISBN 0-85292-461-5

Phototypeset by Paragon Photoset, Aylesbury
Printed in Great Britain by The Cromwell Press,
Broughton Gifford, Wiltshire.

Note: wherever appropriate the convention has been followed
whereby *he* and *him* are used to cover *she* and *her*.

INSTITUTE OF PERSONNEL
AND DEVELOPMENT

IPD House, Camp Road, London SW19 4UX
Tel: 0181 946 9100   Fax: 0181 947 2570
Registered office as above. Registered Charity No. 1038333
A company limited by guarantee. Registered in England No. 2931892

Contents

David Clutterbuck, co-founder and chairman of the ITEM Group plc, a business communications company, is an international management writer and speaker. His previous management books include the best-selling *The Winning Streak*, *The Marketing Edge* and *The Decline and Rise of British Industry*.

He contributes regularly to a variety of management publications and is European editor of Tom Peters's *On Achieving Excellence*.

Marion Devine is a graduate of Reading University. She specializes in writing on issues concerning women and employment.

Helen Beech is a freelance writer with a public relations background and a former corporate communications executive at the ITEM Group plc.

Chapter 1
Mentoring as an alternative method of career development

To some, mentoring is a new and highly effective means of identifying and developing high-flyers; to others it is a means of speeding and facilitating the induction of young people in general. It can also be seen as an effective door into middle and senior management for those subject to unfair discrimination. Finally, some people see it as a dangerous process that can amplify favouritism and exclusive networks within the corporation. Although mentoring was a largely unknown term until the late 1960s, it has become the subject of intense academic study and widespread experimentation, particularly in the United States.

The word 'mentor' originally comes from Greek mythology. Ulysses, before setting out on an epic voyage, entrusted his son to the care and direction of his old and trusted friend Mentor. Yet in spite of the variety of definitions of mentoring (and the variety of names given to it, from coaching or counselling to sponsorship) all the experts and communicators appear to agree that modern mentoring has its origins in the concept of apprenticeship. In the days when the guilds ruled the commercial world, the road to the top in business began in an early apprenticeship to the master craftsman, a trader, or a ship's captain. This older, more experienced, individual passed down his knowledge of how the task was done and how to operate in the commercial world.

Intimate personal relationships frequently developed between the master (or mentor) and the apprentice (or protégé), especially as the apprentice acquired skills and began to substitute for his mentor. Marrying the master's daughter became an accepted means of providing career progression and retaining key skills with the firm.

The Industrial Revolution altered this emphasis, demanding

1

large numbers of recruits which swamped personalized attention. Apprenticeship often degenerated to the stage where it involved depersonalized mass training in technical areas. Within the large corporation there grew up informal, often hidden methods of passing on the experience of old – timers to young recruits. At the lower levels, a supervisor might 'keep an eye on' a promising employee. Senior managers might identify a potential high–flyer and provide him with confidential advice and encouragement. Therefore, although the term may not have had currency, mentoring was nonetheless at work.

The problem with this informal arrangement, which is now commonplace throughout the business world, is that it can be highly arbitrary. The mentor may choose a protégé because he is related, because he reminds him of himself 20 years before, or for any other of a dozen reasons that have no relationship to actual or potential performance. Promotion often becomes unduly influenced by 'old boy' networks that operate by invitation only. Sometimes referred to derisively and with some truth as a corporate godfather, the mentor may exert a power of suffrage and extract fealty.

Discussion of the pros and cons of the mentoring relationship began with one Ralph M Stodgill who referred to the mentor in the late 1960s as 'an ambiguous authority figure'. Daniel Levinson, 10 years later, in a study of 40 mentoring relationships, described him as 'a mixture of parent and peer. His primary function is to be a transitional figure in a man's development'. He calls mentoring 'one of the most complex and developmentally important relationships a man can have in early adulthood'. Other communicators refer to the mentor as 'a role model . . . a guide, a tutor, a coach and a confidant'. In the words of Agnes Missirian, Professor of Management at Bentley College in Waltham, Massachusetts, 'there is a very strong emotional bond and, according to research, personal identification with the mentor as distinct from a sponsor'.

Dr Audrey Collin, of the School of Management at Leicester Polytechnic, gathered a number of definitions of mentoring for an article in *Industrial and Commercial Training* magazine. Mentors were said, for example, to be 'influential people who significantly help you reach your major life goals'. Mentoring is 'a process in which one person [mentor] is responsible for overseeing the career and development of another person [protégé] outside the normal manager/subordinate relationship'. Alternatively, mentoring is 'a protected relationship in which learning and experimentation can occur, potential skills can be developed, and in which results can be measured in terms of competencies gained rather than curricular territory covered'.

Aware that the mentoring relationship can be highly beneficial for those who participate, various companies on both sides of the Atlantic have sought to formalize it. Their objective is to ensure that this valuable developmental tool is used for the good of the company as a whole, rather than for a small number of favourites.

Most of these companies have focused their schemes on potential high-flyers. Others have tried to give all new entrants at certain levels a helping hand from above. All would agree with this description of the mentoring process contained in a 1978 *Harvard Business Review* article entitled 'Everyone who makes it has a mentor':

> Young people shall be given their heads, to challenge the organization to grow. These young people will also have an older person in the organization to look after them in their early years to ensure that their careers get off to a good start. Out of these relationships it is hoped that the young people learn to take risks, accept a philosophical commitment to sharing and learn to relate to people in an intuitive, empathetic way.

These companies have realized that employee development and career progression, particularly at management levels, can be faster and more beneficial to both the individual and the company if a more senior manager spares the time to tutor his juniors. Gerald Roche's study in 1979, 'Much Ado About Mentoring', showed that of the executives he had studied, those with mentors were happier with their career progress and took more pleasure from their work.

Many senior executives of very large firms make a practice of being present for a few hours at junior management training courses. They recognize that close encounters with top management are an important part of induction to the management hierarchy. Mentoring, however, goes

far beyond this fleeting presence. It involves an intense
commitment, by both mentor and protégé, to active career
development. It is demanding in time and in emotional
resources. It requires exceptional and sustained effort not
for a few weeks, but for a minimum of a year and on average
two or three years. It is, in short, to the normal management
methods what Cayenne pepper is to mixed spice.

Mentoring underwent a rapid expansion in the United
States in the late 1970s and early 1980s and has shown similar
expansion in the UK in the late 1980s. However, most of
the research tends to have been carried out in the original
US firms. Research in the UK has been largely confined
to surveys and short case studies. Part of the appeal of the
concept is that it makes use of networks and resources that
already exist and operate within the firm. Part is also that,
in a time of increasing strain on training and development
resources, anything that pushes the burden of developing
managerial talent back onto the more experienced managers
and away from the training department is seen as a good
thing.

It is also asserted (if unproven) that mentoring is a more
efficient form of developing talent. One piece of supporting
evidence for this is that in many cases the relationship forces
the mentor to develop as well, so in effect the company is
training two people for the price of one. It is also widely
claimed that people who have been mentored reach senior
positions, on average, two years ahead of those who have
not.

The price, however, should not be underestimated. The
time investment by all parties involved, including the
personnel department, is substantial. Once started, the
process cannot be easily stopped without bringing into
question the genuineness of the company's commitment to
developing managerial talent. It therefore pays to prepare
even a pilot mentoring scheme with great thoroughness, and
to think through the degree of commitment the company
and the individuals likely to be involved can actually afford
to give.

It also pays to consider at whom a mentoring scheme is
aimed. Most schemes have as their primary aim the provision
of a steady supply of broadly experienced, capable middle and
senior managers. Putting people through such a scheme who

do not have the ability to scale the corporate heights can be a recipe for creating frustrated ambition.

On the other hand, people who do not have the ability to reach middle and senior management can still benefit greatly from mentoring. A good mentoring programme should help people recognize their abilities and limitations, help them seize opportunities and come to terms with the reality of their career potential. Indeed the person destined to remain in a supervisory or junior management role may well need more personalized attention, encouragement and advice than the person who sees a clear career progression ahead of him. A handful of companies have therefore adopted dual mentoring programmes that cater for both kinds of employee.

A good mentoring relationship is one where mentor and protégé have mutual respect, recognize their need for personal development and have at least some idea of where they both want to go. Agnes Missirian defines the ideal relationship as one where the mentor is confident enough not to perceive the protégé as a threat and the protégé has sufficient respect for the mentor that he is willing to accept observations and criticisms he doesn't want to hear. Most successful mentoring relationships blossom into friendships that continue long after the need for tutoring has passed. Tony Milne of CEPEC at Sundridge Park Management Centre goes so far as to describe mentoring as 'best understood as a form of love relationship . . . it can offer great satisfactions to mentor and protégé alike'. At the same time, because it is such a personal relationship and because many people still feel it has conferred upon them special advantages, there is often considerable reluctance to be identified as a protégé. For this reason, many of the examples quoted in the following chapters, though real, are anonymous.

In most cases, there will be eight to 15 years between the mentor and his protégé(s). The most common arrangement will be between a graduate, a junior manager, supervisor or raw business school recruit and a middle manager. However, mentoring does occur between top management and junior management (IBM and Sainsbury are just two of many companies where the chief executive attaches a very junior manager to his office to learn the ropes of corporate governance).

Mentoring may also occur between top management and middle management, particularly where promising people have risen up the hierarchy in only one function or one division of the company.

Moreover, mentoring need not be a once in a lifetime occurrence. Many people experience a succession of mentoring relationships as they pass through different stages in their careers. It seems that the determined individual, who chooses his employers carefully and recognizes the value of a friend at the right court can usually find a mentor whether under a formal or an informal scheme. That mentor may be his immediate boss but as we shall discuss in chapter 5 and in the conclusion, mentoring frequently works better if the roles of mentor and boss are not confused, not least because the two roles can on occasion be contradictory. Hence most formal mentoring schemes, and those upon which this book is focused, concentrate on the relationship between the junior employee and a more senior individual above and usually to the side of his boss. However, the range of applications of mentoring is wide and includes:

- Young graduate recruits – for example, Cable and Wireless appoints mentors from middle management for the two-year duration of its graduate induction programme.
- Young professionals seeking qualifications – for example, brewers such as Bass appoint technical mentors to assist employees studying for master brewer qualifications.
- Junior managers moving into middle management – for example, private hospital group AMI has a mentoring programme to assist potential high-flyers into general management posts.
- Middle managers aspiring to the board – for example, Trafalgar House's advanced management development programme appoints senior management mentors to assist middle managers through a four-year action learning MBA.
- Disadvantaged groups – some US companies use mentoring as a means of bringing women and racial minorities into the management structure. There are proposals in the UK to use mentoring to encourage the development of more black solicitors.

In the following chapters we will look at the recent growth of mentoring, how mentoring works, the benefits to the company, the mentor and the protégé, and how to avoid some of the problems inherent in formalizing mentoring within the organization.

Chapter 2
Mentoring in the past decade

The US, where mentoring first became a serious issue for management discussion and study, continues to have a large number of programmes. Some organizations have discontinued programmes, however – the result, it appears, of over-enthusiastic, poorly managed schemes that failed to achieve their potential.

In the UK, however, the pace of growth of mentoring has increased in the mid to late 1980s. A survey, carried out jointly by the Industrial Society and the ITEM Group in late 1989 found that forty-four out of one hundred and forty-five responding organizations had mentoring programmes of some description; of these, 70% had been started within the previous five years and 27% within two years.

A 1987 study of mentoring in eight countries – Australia, France, Germany, Holland, Ireland, Spain, the United States and the United Kingdom – found that a third of schemes were pilots, and up to 40% in some countries. Just under half of all schemes had been running for two years or less. One scheme in five had been in operation for ten years or more.

Among key conclusions of the survey were:

- most schemes were used 'to develop young professionals'
- British and Australian companies were most receptive to the concept of a formal mentoring programme. Even at this stage, US companies were tending more towards the informal approach
- few schemes had been discontinued and 93% of companies expected their schemes to carry on. Where mentoring had failed, the main reason was inadequate training for the mentors
- the main impediments to a successful scheme were reported

as 'time commitment for mentors, company culture and resistance from top management'.

Typical of the range of British schemes are the following:

- Pilkington Glass introduced its scheme in the mid 1980s, in large part as an inducement to attract high-calibre graduates. The company, which has since extended its scheme to non-graduates, was particularly concerned to minimize the waste and loss of reputation that occurs when graduates leave – it calculates the average expenditure, including salary, training and investment of management time on each graduate at about £60,000.
- AMI Healthcare, which stresses the importance of involving senior management in all training and development activities, saw mentoring as a natural step in the development process of an organization where managers are given considerable autonomy and held to be ultimately responsible for their decisions.
- Many of the District, Unit and Regional General Managers at the NHS in Wales are products of mentoring, which is the cornerstone of their management training programme.
- The Brewers Society has established a tutoring mentor scheme for people studying to become master brewers. The scheme was initiated in large part by the success of a similar programme at Bass Brewing. Says a spokesman for Bass: 'We make sure everyone has an experienced mentor – a brewer in the same plant. He gives guidance, help and gentle backside kicking. The signs are that the scheme is working – the percentage of rate of pass first time round has rocketed in ball park terms from 60% to 90%.'
- Cable and Wireless has a graduate mentoring scheme, aimed at speeding up the integration of graduate recruits into the operations of an international company. The scheme is a major plank of the overall induction and management development programmes. After nine months, the graduate trainees are posted around the world, some to as far away as Hong Kong. Each mentoring pair decides upon its own method of handling this separation. Some rely on long, regular telephone calls; others on a surrogate mentor in the overseas region; yet others combine the two

approaches. Most relationships survive their temporary separation, which lasts nine months, remarkably well.

Not all UK programmes are a success, however. One large UK retailing company initiated a campaign to create mentors in every one of its branches. However, it provided little or no central support for this initiative and such mentoring as happened two years later was spasmodic, informal and unrewarded. Most staff did not even know the programme existed.

Such failures in support are commonplace, unfortunately. One company in the Industrial Society/ITEM survey had introduced a scheme, then promptly changed the organizational structure, putting so much pressure for operational results on the mentors that they had no time to spare for building the relationship with their protégés. The scheme did not even get off the ground, and the company switched its attention to a new fad, interactive video, with much the same inadequate level of preparation.

The Industrial Society/ITEM survey found that relatively few companies with mentoring schemes gave mentors formal training, although more than half offered some form of support, mostly through workshops and regular meetings of mentors to exchange views and discuss problems. By contrast, only 11% of companies that use managers formally for coaching (a key skill for mentors) provided relevant training for all or most of the managers involved. Slightly less than half of organizations with formal programmes of career counselling (another important mentoring role) provided training and only one company trained all of its managers in career counselling. The picture that emerges, therefore, is one of growing enthusiasm, but frequently without the support that schemes need to be a real success.

The United States has already encountered the problems that result from such failures. In a seminal article entitled, 'Take my mentor, please', management journalist Peter Kizilos reports: 'The value of the ancient master-apprentice relationship had been recognized by post-industrial theoreticians. The secret to success wasn't found in some new-fangled seminar. Advancement depended on finding a high-muck-a-muck who would adopt you like a son or daughter.'

In practice, however, he says, high expectations by

protégés (victims of hype by both the business media and over-enthusiastic researchers and consultants) have been compounded by corporations that undervalue personal and professional development, and which often see formal mentoring programmes as a quick fix. He quotes Michael Zey, a veteran writer on mentoring: 'Managers will say, "Let's draft a few people to be in the program. Let's link them up and bring in a speaker to talk about mentoring." Then they go off and leave the mentors and protégés on their own.'

Current opinion on mentoring in the US appears to be polarizing between the 'traditionalists', who have made a success of formal programmes, through thorough preparation and strong involvement of both line managers and the training department; and the proponents of informal mentoring. The latter agree that 'true mentor-protégé relationships are rare. They must develop naturally, not at gun-point.' Forced coupling can fuel discontent, anger, resentment and suspicion. The critics argue that a more effective approach is for people to establish a *network of mentors* – a conclusion supported by a 1984 survey of seven thousand managers at Honeywell Inc in Minneapolis.

Successful US mentoring programmes started more recently have tended to steer a middle path. Kizilos cites the Kansas City office of the US Internal Revenue Service, which installed a programme in May 1989. In this scheme, the protégés are newly appointed first-line supervisors; the mentors are senior managers, who have been trained to carry out the role. The managers are all screened volunteers, who join a pool of mentors. While the training department makes recommendations, compatibility is decided by the protégés and mentors themselves, often via social gatherings where they can meet informally.

The success of the IRS programme is attributed partly to the relatively relaxed nature of the match-making, and partly to the management climate. According to Filomena Warihay, the consultant working with the organization, a strong acceptance by line managers of the value of developing younger managers (backed up, if possible, by an established career development planning process) is an essential prerequisite for success.

In the UK, a number of organizations are following similar

reasoning. A large educational institution, for example, recognizing that there will be little direct support from the top for a formal, highly structured mentoring programme, is assessing instead an informal scheme, in which mentors are trained and sent in search of suitable protégés. A financial services company is looking to including mentoring as a core skill in its development programme for *all* managers. Mentor-protégé relationships will be brought about by suggestions from the training department, from line managers or at the request of would-be protégés.

Whether formal or informal, successful UK schemes fail to recognize the need for continuous monitoring or review. Slightly more than half of the companies in the Industrial Society/ITEM survey used a coordinator to watch for problems and to bring about improvements. One in four regularly interviewed the mentors and protégés, while two organizations carried out periodic attitude surveys.

In the rest of this book we will continue to draw upon these surveys, and upon the specific experience of UK companies, as a source of lessons, which may help future programmes avoid pitfalls and maximize the potential of what remains an extremely valuable management development tool.

Chapter 3
How mentoring benefits the individual

Every company needs some form of career development programme to produce a succession of motivated, upward-moving employees. Even employees who are destined to remain at the same level may need career development as the jobs they are in change or become obsolete. Managers with high potential should identify and improve their skills, set career goals and know how to achieve those goals in the most practical and efficient way. Conventional career development courses provide some of the answers, but all too often fail to provide adequate follow up. The results, too, are often hard to define. Schemes involving selection by assessment centres of high-flyers or frequent job rotation to gain wide experience probably offer the nearest thing to tangible results, but are extremely expensive, not least because at each change the young person has to start again at the beginning of the learning cycle of the new job.

Leaving career development solely to managers, while cheaper, tends to be singularly ineffective. A manager may lack the ability to recognize a potential high-flyer or, if he does, be reluctant to lose that employee by counselling him to move to another area of the company. Managers who are unavailable, uncommitted, or who dislike particular subordinates can effectively block the career paths of talented employees and prevent them from realizing their potential.

A mentoring programme, as a formal method of recognizing talent in a company, is a viable alternative to both these approaches. It can be carried out in tandem with traditional career development methods and has reasonably good predictability in its results. It may be run for as long as the employee benefits from it. As in many other relationships, both protégé and mentor have to work hard to make it succeed; both can draw substantial benefits.

The benefits to the protégé

1 Easier induction for those coming straight from university or moving to a new country

(a) One mentor comments: 'Mentoring is a means of smoothing out graduates' transition from an educational environment – one of the major changes of their life – and enabling them to settle in more quickly'. According to the NHS in Wales, it 'provides exceptional opportunities and the unique status of having someone to trust in a bewildering environment', who can direct the protégé's learning opportunities.

(b) A French protégé working in England stresses how important her mentor has been: 'My mentor has worked abroad and can speak French. He has helped me to adapt to the British way of life. The scheme has definitely helped me to settle into this country and the company.'

(c) Chemical company Hoescht has a dozen or so British apprentices in its German operations. Although they have a tutor in the UK, they are also assigned German mentors to relieve the isolation they can feel and to provide career counselling.

2 Improved self confidence

(a) The protégé gains a sense of self-worth and importance. The one-to-one relationship between the mentor and the protégé helps the latter feel that the company values him as an individual rather than as a cog in the managerial wheel. A mentor gives protégés (in particular graduates) undergoing frequent job rotation and management change a point of stability in what may seem an unpredictable environment. By helping them explore their own potential, the mentor also enables them to gain the self-knowledge so necessary for well-founded self-confidence.

  For example, one of ICI's reasons for starting its mentoring programme was to help university recruits adapt to business life.

3 Learning to cope with the formal and informal structure of the company

(a) Through the mentor, the protégé learns about the formal culture of an organization, its values, its company image, objectives and predominant management style.

(b) The mentor advises the protégé on self presentation and behaviour so that he can fit into the company's formal culture. The protégé learns how to publicize himself within the organization, when to be noticed as an individual and when to be seen working collaboratively.

(c) A protégé learns how to operate successfully within the informal culture. The mentor helps the protégé work his way through the internal company politics by identifying for him the key decision-makers in the company and which executives have the real power. As one senior executive comments: 'If you do not know the rules of the game, you cannot operate. The only way to know these rules is to be invited by an insider to participate.'

4 Career advice and advancement

(a) A mentor can act as a role model to the protégé. The mentor is a tangible symbol of what the protégé can achieve in the future and helps the protégé to focus his career aspirations and turn them into realistic objectives.

(b) The protégé learns how to move quickly up the promotion ladder. As a senior executive, the mentor has a direct knowledge and experience of the career structure of the company. The mentor advises the protégé on which jobs to take and when to take them. Jenny Blake, an industrial consultant, adds: 'My job was easy, well paid, near my home, undemanding and well below my full capacity. I was offered a marketing job with Shell, which I was reluctant to take because I wanted to stay with my mentor. When I told him this, he said that if I stayed he would make me redundant. He was not nasty, but he wanted to show me that I was taking the easy way out. He was trying to help me to take control of my life and face these important career decisions.'

A female protégé in the social services was advised by her mentor to apply for a position she felt was unattainable.

She comments: 'Before the internal interviews my mentor kept dropping my name to other senior administrative officers. He also frequently mentioned me to his own superior. Two other people in the department also applied for the vacancy. There was a woman on my level who had four years' experience and a man a grade higher. Everyone was very surprised when I got the promotion, since it was virtually unknown for someone of my age and experience to jump three levels.'

Sometimes the mentor may suggest a total reorientation of career direction and may recommend a decrease or increase in the pace of advancement. One young manager recalls his attitude before he had a mentor:

> I was never sure about the timing of my career; when I should try to move upward or when I should stay in one position. I thought I ought to understand a job completely before I applied for promotion. Then a senior executive took an interest in my career and told me that if I stayed too long in one job I would probably get stuck there since I would not be recognized as a high flyer. He advised me to apply for a post two grades above my current one. I didn't think I'd get it, but I did.

(c) A protégé gains a higher profile with his mentor. A mentor increases the visibility of the protégé to executive levels by frequently describing how well his charge is progressing. The mentor may involve the protégé in his own projects and bring him into executive meetings, inviting him to speak up on the areas he has covered. The mentor will brief him beforehand on how to present himself and give him background on other subjects scheduled to be discussed.

4 Managerial tutorage

(a) A protégé gains an insight into management processes through observing his mentor closely. The mentor provides an example of effective management and successful leadership and so accelerates the protégé's learning pace. An American protégé at Unisys comments:

A mentor teaches the invaluable lesson of people management to a protégé who is often straight out of management school. He may know all about cost-benefit analysis and be an economic wizard, but he needs to be shown, for example, the importance of building support teams. A mentor has the experience to teach this.

A British protégé agrees, explaining: 'When mentoring works, it minimizes the period during which one learns from mistakes. As a graduate, you feed off someone else and so the learning processes are speeded up.' John Chadwick, now Director of Sundridge Park Management Centre, remembers his experience as a protégé at the Glacier Metal Company: 'Before long we were exchanging notes on the shop floor experiences I was soaking in, comparing our assessment of abilities. All the time I was extending and testing my critical faculties. Towards the end of the session, he would always share with me his own problems and uncertainties. He would explain the process of resolving situations, the stress of decisions and the excellence of success. All the time he was infecting me with the management virus.'

(b) A mentor is able to use his influence in the organization to facilitate the protégé's access to areas otherwise closed to him. As a result, the protégé better understands how the organization functions. Interviews with 'graduated' protégés reveal that one of the most valuable parts of the relationship is frequent discussion of how the business works and why middle and senior management do not do things the way the protégé would. John Chadwick adds: 'As an engineer trained in logic, I found this world of compromise, choice and timing initially mysterious. Then, as my mentor's advice bore fruits, it became less of a mystery and more of a challenge to read the organization. Rapidly I became able to discuss with him strengths and weaknesses in other managers, and ways in which they could be approached to form a working relationship. The blindly obvious shortcomings of the business seemed less idiotic when put by him into the context of the broader market.'

(c) A protégé has a legitimate source of advice and information in the mentor. For example, Jenny Blake found 'it was very difficult to sell to the Middle East, especially since I was a woman and not allowed to go there. My mentor was in charge of the Middle East marketing section and was able to give me invaluable advice. He made me aware of important cultural differences and expectations when I was dealing with foreign marketing representatives, for instance, how they expected to be treated with respect and to be made a fuss of.' A junior manager describes the problem he faced without such a figure: 'Often a young manager has to try to gather information without betraying his ignorance. It is a very risky business. To get ahead you have to supply the right answers and not ask the wrong questions.' In a mentor-protégé relationship, the protégé can ask naïve questions in an unthreatening atmosphere. Helen Martin, a mentor at BP Chemicals, feels 'a mentor is not an agony aunt or a miracle cure for all problems. We are simply people who have probably experienced similar situations in the past. We can therefore help the individual to find the best way to tackle an issue themselves.'

5 Benefits for the less talented employee

The less gifted employee who has the benefit of a mentoring relationship need not gain less from it. His job satisfaction may be increased by an understanding of how to work within his limitations and how to broaden the current job, ie to seek challenge horizontally rather than vertically. He will need the same skills of handling people, or of teamwork and the same knowledge of how the organization functions to achieve lesser aims.

The benefits to the mentor

1 Improved job satisfaction

(a) Grooming a promising young employee can be a challenging and stimulating experience for a mentor, especially if his own career has reached a temporary or permanent plateau. A spokesman for Pilkington Glass says: 'Some managers, whose careers have reached a real or perceived plateau, found the challenge of mentoring both rewarding and stimulating. This change may even have a longer-term effect on their own career prospects.'

(b) Mentors often find the mentoring relationship rewarding in many other ways, for example in the sense of pride when the protégé performs well. Mentors also gain a sense of purpose in seeing the values and culture of an organization handed to a new generation and in thinking more carefully about company policies. Pilkington Glass mentors comment: 'Mentoring has made us question traditional thinking and practices, firstly to clarify them in our own minds before explaining them to our protégés, but also in not just defending them when challenged through the innocent, unadulterated eyes of the newcomer who has not yet been influenced by our culture.'

(c) Mentors learn from the relationship, too. The process of climbing the corporate ladder often means missing out on new ideas, techniques and technologies. There never seems to be the time for catching up and at a certain stage it becomes embarrassing to admit ignorance. Directing the learning experiences of the protégé gives the mentor the excuse he needs to devote the time to developing his own knowledge, too. It is also often acknowledged that the best way to learn is to teach.

Some companies, among them AMI Healthcare, see protégés as a source of practical help for the mentor, while Midland Bank has found that 'mentors have identified a need to increase their own business awareness of Midland Group in order to be better placed to respond to protégés'.

(d) Some mentors use their protégés as 'robot arms' to accomplish at a distance and less publicly what they cannot do directly from their more visible position in middle or senior management. This applies particularly to information gathering and the initiation of new projects.

(e) Mentoring can give the mentor a different perspective on the company and keep him in touch with grassroot feelings.

(f) Mentors often learn how to relate better with other graduates that they line manage.

2 Increased peer recognition

(a) A mentor who identifies promising employees acquires
    a reputation for having a keen insight into the needs
    of the company. This enhances his status with his
    peers.
        The international accounting firm Merrill, Lynch,
    Pierce, Fenner & Smith has constructed a formal system
    of rewarding its mentors. Mentors' names are included in
    regularly circulated reports about protégés' accom-
    plishments. Mentors are personally thanked by top
    management and are invited to be presenters at mentor
    briefing sessions, which are run for new participants. A
    spokesman for the firm explains: 'We feel we need to
    reward our mentors visibly and link their success publicly
    to the success of the mentoring programme.'
        At AMI Healthcare the status of mentor is a public
    recognition of skills and expertise.

3 Career advancement

(a) The mentor can ease his work load by delegating projects to
    managers he has personally trained through a mentoring
    programme. He can control the quality of the work since
    he knows which areas his protégés are especially skilled in
    and knows how they will approach the task. As a result,
    his own efficiency is increased.
(b) Part of the motivation to be a mentor is the opportunity
    to increase personal reputation by being surrounded by
    talented and upward-moving managers. This in turn
    attracts other bright managers who believe the mentor
    offers them the best hope of advancement in the com-
    pany.
(c) A mentor benefits from the energy and enthusiasm of his
    protégés. He also receives new ideas and perspectives
    by allowing the protégés to be involved in his own
    work.
(d) A mentor can assist his own promotion prospects by
    grooming his protégé to be his successor. In this way
    he may overcome the frequent problem of becoming
    entrenched in one position because his company feels
    he is irreplaceable. One observer comments: 'The only

way of getting promoted yourself is by identifying your successor.' On the other hand, the mentor can have a powerful future ally in his protégé if the latter outstrips him in his career.

(e) The mentor also has a useful contact in the protégé should he realize all his potential and develop his own extensive network of useful contacts.

(f) One thing the mentor does not receive, and should not be led to expect from the scheme, is a direct payment or bonus to compensate him for his time and effort. One argument against such payments is that developing others is an integral part of every manager's job. A more powerful argument is that mentorship has to be built on friendship and is a close and personal relationship. Hence, turning it into a paid service is likely to hinder the relaxed and informal atmosphere necessary between mentor and protégé. In theory, this can become a problem if the company links human development objectives to a bonus scheme as part of the annual performance appraisal. In practice, the trick is to ensure that the mentor is neither especially rewarded nor penalized for this part of his job.

Mentors at Pilkington Glass perceive the following benefits:

- 'We clarify and question our perception of the company
- We see the company through fresh eyes
- We improve our abilities so we have more to offer the protégés
- We see people work in different ways depending on whether they are theorists, activists etc.
- It offers a new challenge
- It offers a new learning experience
- We understand the trauma new recruits experience and can be more sympathetic to others undergoing change.'

The NHS in Wales, on the other hand, describes the benefits to a mentor as:

- 'A fresh challenge
- Satisfaction from seeing his charge progress
- Knowing he is contributing to the company's future.'

What the surveys say

The 1987 PA international survey found that the most common benefit for companies from mentoring was 'improved succession planning and management development', followed by faster induction of new employees and better communications. Reduced training costs, increased productivity and reduced labour costs also figured, to a lesser extent.

The most important benefits for protégés, says the PA survey, were 'personal support' and 'teaching and counselling'. Other benefits recorded were 'career planning', 'knowledge and awareness of the company', 'role modelling' and 'commitment to the company'.

Mentors, on the other hand, gained primarily 'psychic rewards' such as pride and a feeling of self-fulfilment and 'job enrichment'. 'Career enhancement' and 'status' were significantly less important except, for some reason, in Australia.

Far and away the main benefit for mentors, according to three-fifths of the companies in another study by the Industrial Society and the ITEM Group, is job enrichment. Status, job interest for plateaued managers and career enhancement are significantly less common primary benefits. Neither survey identified any organization which pays its mentors, although some companies clearly use development of more junior employees as an important element in performance appraisal and in assessing managers' suitability for promotion.

Summary

Mentoring holds out considerable benefits for both the mentor and the protégé. It enables the protégé to find his feet more quickly and to establish a clear sense of career direction and purpose. It often rejuvenates the mentor and may advance his career, too.

Chapter 4
How mentoring benefits the company

Mentoring can work in most companies, regardless of size, culture, or market sector. It can communicate to employees far more fully the complexity of procedures and the unique nature of the company than any formal training course, induction booklets or company manual.

Mentoring enhances the abilities of both the mentor and protégé, so the organization gains through increased efficiency. Companies with formal, long-standing mentoring programmes claim tangible increases in productivity and efficiency. Intangible benefits include improved staff morale, greater career satisfaction and swifter getting up to speed when mentored managers are inserted into a new job.

Another significant impetus behind mentoring is the cost – not in cash terms (mentoring is NOT a cheap alternative when you take into account the value of senior management time) – but in saving expensive off-site courses, which take employees away from productive activity for weeks on end.

The rewards of a mentoring programme are:

1 recruitment and induction
2 improved motivation
3 a stable corporate culture
4 leadership development
5 improved communications.

1 Easier recruitment and induction

A formal mentoring programme eases the sometimes difficult process of assimilating new recruits. Pilkington Glass, for example, has found graduate induction has become less of an ordeal since it began mentoring. Enthusiasm has been productively channelled and graduates are taking on greater responsibility as their commitment grows.

Most staff turnover occurs during the first six months with a new employer and a major cause is inability to adjust rapidly enough. Assigning a mentor to a new arrival helps overcome the counter-productive problems of culture shock and the uncertainty most people feel as they find their feet in the new environment. Employees become productive more quickly and are likely to stay with the company longer. A spokesman for Pilkington adds: 'The rewards are that the employee settles down faster in the new job or environment and becomes effective more quickly. Harmony is also maximized.' Pilkington has retained 94% of the graduates who took part in its mentoring programme in recent years.

Hughes Aircraft, for example, wanted to improve the quality of its university intake. It felt that even the top universities lacked an up-to-date knowledge of the industry, so it encouraged its senior scientists to tutor recruits in technical and professional matters. Newcomers now adjust to the new working environment relatively swiftly.

Mentoring also cultivates in the protégé an increased sense of commitment and loyalty to the organization. The mentor is the mediator between the protégé and the company. Through close interaction with the protégé he creates a personal atmosphere in what might otherwise seem a faceless bureaucratic organization. The protégé receives through him a positive perception of the company. Under the guidance of the mentor he gains a clearer sense of his function. The protégé can be made to feel he is participating in the inner operations of the company and this in turn generates in him a closer identification with the organization's goals.

Many companies experience difficulties in attracting the right kind of graduates, even in times of severe unemployment. A mentoring programme can be a significant inducement for graduates to join less glamorous firms or industries, because it demonstrates commitment to management development and staff retention. It is particularly attractive if it offers a fast track to middle management.

In some cases, a mentoring programme starts working for the company even before the new recruits turn up. Jewel Companies, a Chicago food retailing firm, designed a mentoring programme to 'merchandise an unglamorous retailer to bright young MBAs'. A spokesman explains:

> Ours is a hard-working, long hours kind of business, in other words not the type MBAs looking for jobs would put on their list. We wanted to bring into the business a talent level we had not been able to reach. All MBAs expect the track to be fast. Now we can say to them: 'You will get enough attention in the first couple of years for both of us to know if you will succeed.' Using this strategy, we emphasize to MBAs that we groom fast-trackers.

2 Motivation

Mentoring can help reduce managerial and professional turnover at other critical stages, too. Young, ambitious people often undergo a period of frustration and impatience when they realize their progress up the company career ladder is slower than they initially expected. If a protégé has a mentor who is taking an active interest in his career and who explains the reasons for and ways round current blockages, he is more likely to persevere. The mentor helps him understand and recognize the long term plans the company has for him. He also helps the protégé make the most of the learning experiences inherent in his current job that will equip him for more senior positions. Hence mentoring lessens the threat of other companies luring away promising young employees with offers of speedier career advancement.

A mentoring relationship also motivates the middle and senior managers involved and can be a valuable means of delaying 'plateauing'. A mentor is less likely to retire mentally in his job if he is constantly faced with fresh challenges arising from a mentoring relationship. He is forced to clarify and articulate his own ideas about the company's organization and goals in order to explain them to his protégé. He may feel he has to improve his own abilities to justify the protégé's respect. Cultivating potential in the company becomes a significant opportunity for him to demonstrate that the old dog is still capable of learning and showing new tricks.

As a result, the mentor may find new purpose and interest in his job.

IBM uses mentoring as a way of giving recognition to middle and senior management while simultaneously showing the protégé what the positions they aspire to would entail. Explains a company spokesman:

> We identify promising managers early in their careers and assign them to a 12 to 18 month tour of duty with senior executives. This relieves the executive of a considerable administrative trivia and widens the young assistant's skills. It is also a good opportunity for the executive to talent spot and gain an accurate idea of the quality of the manager.

3 A stable corporate culture

A mentoring programme ensures that managerial skills are accurately transferred from senior to junior levels. The protégé can observe and emulate closely the methods his mentor uses for getting things done. Even if the protégé decides to develop his own managerial methods, he can understand the corporate values beneath the mentor's management style. At AMI Healthcare, existing links between protégés and mentors (who are members of the senior management group) mean that if a protégé is promoted his integration is often smoother because he has been well prepared and has someone he knows well to refer to.

Michael Zey, author of *The Mentor Connection*, refers to the example of a general manager of merchandising who was mentored by a vice-president. The mentor demonstrated to her that the most successful way of managing staff was 'not by authority, but by commanding respect, by showing that you try to do your best and that you respect other people'.

Transmitting the corporate culture also decreases the likelihood of tension and friction when a protégé steps up into a more senior position. If the mentoring programme has worked well, the protégé will have been groomed for the job and will have a detailed knowledge of how to handle both peers and subordinates, some of whom may feel threatened by his promotion.

Another case cited by Zey was a woman newly promoted to junior management in an engineering section. A senior engineer in her department was very aggressive towards her and plainly resented her position. Her mentor suggested to her that this was because the engineer saw her as a threat. He advised her to present herself more as a product manager than as a scientist, and to try to meet frequently with the engineer to discuss product development. This strategy reassured the engineer that his technical position was not under threat and the relationship eventually became cordial and co-operative.

The smooth transfer of the company culture between one generation of managers and the next provides a degree of stability that both *In Search of Excellence* and its derivatives have shown to be a key factor in long-term corporate growth and survival. This continuity also allows the company to absorb sudden changes in leadership without losing the focus of its objectives. Because mentors frequently mould their protégés into personal replacements, this sense of continuity continues right down the management line.

This dimension of mentoring can be especially important for small or medium sized companies undergoing a change of ownership. The company's market value is frequently related to its ability to function without problems after the founder has left. An effective mentoring programme ensures the company does not lose direction or purpose during this period.

Even at the lower levels in the organization mentoring can help establish a common understanding of the company's objectives and values that facilitates communication in the workplace. The relationship may be less intense, the impact in individual cases less noticeable, but the potential benefits in terms of workforce co-operation are considerable.

4 Leadership development

Besides teaching managerial and personnel skills, mentoring reveals to the protégé how power is gained and wielded within the company. This is frequently a crucial lesson and is one of the most powerful sources of motivation for a young manager. A business school education may teach valuable theoretical skills but it cannot normally teach a manager how to exercise and feel comfortable with power; nor can it give him the confidence to make a major deal on his own initiative, take calculated risks or launch a new product.

Spending large amounts of corporate money can be an intimidating experience for a newly promoted manager. Another of Zey's cases highlights:

> You cannot teach someone to spend two million dollars through a formal method. So as not to overwhelm my protégé I first start by expressing all financial sums in single units, and teach him to make decisions on little things while keeping in mind the long term costs. He gradually learns how to manipulate resources and feel more comfortable with power.

5 Improved communications

The protégé's unique position in the organization can aid informal communications because he straddles several levels. For example, through the relationship with the mentor the junior management protégé has access to and is accepted by middle and senior management. At the same time he is accepted in the lower managerial levels. Since he is familiar with the language and mannerisms of both, he can efficiently communicate each group's ideas and opinions to the other. Rich informal communication networks improve productivity and efficiency in a company since they lead to more action, more innovation, more learning and swifter adjustment to changing business needs. It can be lonely at the top. The chance to pass information to lower levels of management restores interdependence between management levels and eases the flow of ideas and information. This special communication network also facilitates easier working of other areas of management development.

Mentoring can sometimes benefit an organization in unexpected ways, too. In one company a protégé was being mentored with the ultimate objective of helping him leave. A spokesman explained:

This highly talented individual has gone as far as is possible in this company. We have no appropriate position for him so we are grooming him to take over a small corporation outside this company. In the meantime, for the three to five years that he stays with us, we benefit from his productivity and enthusiasm. In the future we will have a very useful ally.

A similar case arose in the North-West region of ICI's engineering department. The company explains:

A sponsored mechanical engineering student began training with us and met her mentor for about three hours on her first day. Two weeks later, she left us and decided to go up to university, forsaking her engineering ambitions. During this time the mentor had provided support, primarily in a counselling mode, to a person living away from home for the first time, in a strange environment. He helped her rethink her ambitions and come to a decision on her future.

The Industrial Society/ITEM Group survey of British companies in 1989 compared expected with actual benefits of mentoring. It found that the primary reason for introducing a mentoring scheme into UK companies was to support a self-development programme (30%), followed by faster induction (26%) and increased retention of staff (20%). Improved identification of potential was the main reason for 14% of companies. Other reasons mentioned were 'ensuring professional qualifications are maintained' and 'development for the mentor'.

When asked what the primary benefits had proved to be in reality, a slightly different picture emerges. Both 'supporting a self-development programme' and 'faster induction' become significantly less important, while 'building relationships', which did not figure at all as the top expected benefit, becomes the primary benefit in one in six cases.

What are the main reasons for using mentoring?

	first	second	third
	(percentages, N=44)		
Induct more quickly	26	9	5
Improved identification of potential	14	18	11
Supporting a self-development programme	30	16	14
Building relationships	0	25	14
Increased retention of key staff	20	7	11
Other	7	9	9
N/A	7	16	36

What are the most important benefits you have found?

	first	second	third
	(percentages, N=44)		
Induct more quickly	9	7	7
Improved identification of potential	9	14	14
Supporting self-development programmes	21	30	7
Building relationships	16	22	18
Increased retention of key staff	20	7	16
Other	11	2	7
N/A	14	18	31

Summary

Mentoring benefits the company through speedier induction and through enhancements in recruitment, motivation and communications. It helps ensure that key cultural values are passed on and allows the company to prepare young people for leadership.

Chapter 5
Choosing the mentor

In theory, every manager's job should entail a significant amount of subordinate development and indeed some companies, such as Siemens, make it a virtual condition of each manager's advancement. In practice, however, some people are better cut out for it than others. Moreover, the ability to act as a mentor will often vary according to the manager's own stage of career development. For example, someone who has only been in middle or senior management himself for a short time may not have enough broad experience to offer. Or someone seeking or undergoing a major change in his own career development is unlikely to have the mental energy to spare for someone else's problem.

In selecting the mentor a company must have a clear sense of the qualities which make a good developer of other people's leadership potential. These qualities may differ from company to company, even from division to division. Equally, the ideal mentor for one person may be a disaster for another. It follows, naturally, that companies will disagree on the criteria they use to identify good mentors. Gerald O'Callaghan of BP Chemicals states: 'Mentors are not picked for any superhuman qualities – though some may fall into that category. Most are experienced, well-balanced professionals and managers who are interested in developing young people and broadening their own contribution to the company. They are among the best staff we have.'

Pilkington Glass looks for a mentor who is accessible, committed, trained, good at nurturing, experienced, influential and not the protégé's line manager. At the North West region of ICI's engineering department, mentors 'are always chartered engineers and are generally junior/middle managers. This same group of people is involved with student and graduate selection, training and management.

Prerequisites are an interest in the training, development and management of people. As well as being receptive to new ideas and open to change, they must be positively critical and challenge the younger person.'

In the rest of this chapter we attempt to set out criteria which most companies with experience of mentoring would agree upon. The one contentious exception is the issue of the relative positions of mentor and protégé. Most companies with mentoring programmes aimed at managers prefer to establish the relationship outside the normal working hierarchy, ie the mentor is normally not the protégé's boss but two or more levels above him either vertically or horizontally. One reason for this is that there are times in the mentoring relationship when both sides need to back off. This is something much easier to do if there is a certain distance between them, either in hierarchical level or departmental function, or both. In addition, the boss/subordinate relationship, with all its entanglements of decisions on pay rises, disciplinary responsibilities and performance appraisal, may work against the openness and candour of the true mentoring relationship. The line manager may also not have a sufficiently wide experience of other job opportunities. Comments from various companies and experts bear out these points.

The programme managers of Trafalgar House Construction Holdings are convinced that an 'uncle' figure is a more appropriate mentor than a line manager. Roger Mills, head of management development, comments: 'The boss has divided loyalties; we are putting him under the wrong pressures. I perceive it particularly when mentors ring me to talk over what they should do where there is a conflict between where the protégé should be for his development needs and where he should be to meet an immediate need from his job.'

Dr Warner Burke, Professor of Psychology at Columbia University, feels 'a mentor should not only be from higher up in the organization, but from a different part of the hierarchy'. Another management development director comments: 'We purposely match our protégés to people who are in different parts of the business and not in the protégés' immediate chain of reporting relationships. We don't want the mentoring relationship to interfere with the supervisory relationship.'

A spokesman for the North West region of ICI's engineering

department says: 'We avoid situations where the mentor acts in a line manager capacity because the roles may become confused. The mentor is responsible for the professional and personal development of the individual and may be seen as accountable to the profession generally and to the institution in particular. The line manager, on the other hand, is responsible to the company for the development of people in order to make better use of them as a resource.'

A protégé from another company states: 'It was very important that I could go to someone who was in a senior position, not directly involved with my work. My mentor opened my eyes to the opportunities available and the knowledge of confidentiality made it all the better.' When BP Chemicals surveyed its protégés it found that some expressed concern at the thought of their line manager's boss becoming their mentor, although most mentors did not seem to have a problem with such a relationship.

In the very broadest terms, the type of managerial training carried out by many retailers, where young people are appointed as assistants to a branch manager who ensures they receive practical experience, can be considered mentoring. By this token, so too could 'sitting by Nellie'. For the purpose of this book we intend to avoid this argument by concentrating on mentoring outside the normal boss/subordinate relationship. The development of staff within the boss/subordinate relationship is a separate issue worthy of a different book.

Because every case is different, the mentor can only be given very general rules on how to deal with the protégé. So one of the key attributes he needs is the ability to respond to individual circumstances and to work out his own strategies for assisting his protégé. So the company must choose individuals who have initiative and are comfortable operating in a career development programme which is largely unstructured.

The general criteria for a good mentor are not necessarily the same as those for a good functional manager. Many firms run into difficulties early on in the programme if they place too much emphasis on an excellent track record as a prerequisite for being a mentor. While the mentor's performance at his job is undeniably important, if only to ensure the protégé's respect, other, equally valuable, skills are also essential. BP Chemicals sees the ideal mentor as 'a professional employee with substantial work experience whose role is to counsel and befriend the new recruit. He or she acts as an impartial but supportive sounding board on all issues that may arise during the graduates' first two years in the company'. A large UK production company points out that power and position should be secondary to character and substance.

A manager who is outstanding in his field may at first glance seem to be an ideal candidate for a mentor. It is just this sort of flair and expertise the company needs to pass on. However, if this manager's communication skills are extremely poor, or he resents being taken from his work because of his mentorship obligations, he is unlikely to function well in the role. The company, the mentor and the protégé may all suffer in these circumstances.

Such a situation arose in one company where the programme co-ordinators attempted to assign mentors to protégés instead of allowing them to volunteer. They picked the most talented employee in research, who reluctantly agreed to act as a mentor. However, the protégé found his mentor was usually inaccessible and rarely spent time with him. The programme co-ordinators were reluctant to assign the protégé to another person for fear of offending his mentor. Trapped by the company politics, the protégé felt his career was being sacrificed to cover up the mistakes of senior management. Not surprisingly, he left to seek his career development elsewhere.

The moral of this story is clear. Companies should choose mentors who can not only communicate their skills well, but who are also actively committed to the programme. Every volunteer mentor is worth a dozen press-ganged. It is not necessary for the mentor to dazzle the protégé with his superior knowledge and experience; he merely has to be able to encourage the protégé by sharing with him his own enthusiasm for his job. The mentor must be ready to invest time and effort into the relationship, so his interests will probably already lie in the areas of communication and interpersonal skills. The mentor must be ready to extend friendship to the protégé and be willing to let the relationship extend beyond the normal limits of a business relationship. He should not participate in the programme unless he is willing to consider the relationship as a long term commitment.

Pilkington Glass sees the mentor as having a number of roles:

- manager of the relationship
- non-threatening adviser
- contact with the protégé's line manager
- training adviser
- tutor.

The Burton Group set out the following criteria for a good mentor. He or she should be able to:

- respond to individual circumstances
- initiate their own strategy
- have good communication skills
- be committed to the mentoring process
- invest time
- have a sound and broad knowledge of the company
- encourage and motivate
- create a continuous learning environment
- achieve mutual respect
- be action-orientated
- have his or her own network of contacts and influence.

These companies avoid people heavily involved in corporate politics, recently established personnel trying to develop their own status, those with a high turnover of staff and those whose staff are of low morale.

In summary, to adopt one commentator's analysis, the mentor must:

Manage the relationship
Encourage the protégé
Nurture the protégé
Teach the protégé
Offer mutual respect
Respond to the protégé's needs.

The mentor who manages

Before he joins a programme, a mentor must be able to assure the company that he can manage both his normal work load and his mentoring relationship. (Indeed, one of the skills he will hope to pass on is effective time management.) Co-ordinators of Merrill Lynch's programme emphasize to the mentor that he must allocate time decisively to his protégé. A spokesman explains: 'Mentoring demands some major time commitments from the mentor, so we want to make sure that they will have the time available and that it will be well spent.'

A mentor should have a wide range of managerial skills rather than be too specialized in one area. The protégé expects the mentor to widen his knowledge of the company, as well as teach him about the different aspects of management. At that stage of his career the protégé needs to know more about the alternatives that are open to him in the company. If he has a mentor who is narrow in his company perspective the protégé can easily be persuaded to follow the mentor's footsteps rather than explore other possibilities which may better fit his potential.

The mentor's rank should not be so much higher than the protégé's that the experience gap becomes a gulf. ICI's engineering department explains: 'It is perhaps for this reason we avoid using senior managers in the mentor role. With the pyramid nature of organizations they ultimately have a line influence. Their seniority can (some would argue should) be intimidating for the young person, who may feel unable to be party to an open relationship, may not seek the desired frequency or level of contact and may not, therefore, develop as effectively as we would wish. Even though the relationship may develop positively, the charge may always hold back for fear of what may happen to an unguarded remark or criticism or a request for help, and it can be difficult for the relationship to develop fruitfully.'

If the protégé is unable to accept and assume at least some of the mentor's perspectives, it will seriously hinder his development rather than assist it. If the mentor is too remote he cannot be involved enough in the day-to-day activities of the protégé sufficiently to understand or discuss his problems. A deputy chairman may in the long term provide sponsorship and promotion, but in the meantime he is probably too far above the protégé to transmit basic skills, which the protégé needs to be a good manager. The protégé will feel discouraged and his self-confidence will not grow with the relationship.

The best mentors are often those who have a sound and seasoned knowledge of the company and its political structure. An individual who is close to retirement should not be chosen to be a mentor merely because he has more spare time than his younger colleagues. Indeed, Agnes Missirian points out that someone who has been with an organization a long time does not necessarily see developing other people as a priority. She suggests that if you give protégés to people out of the mainstream, they can represent all the failed dreams of the person who has been shunted aside.

Rather, candidates should be selected because the company recognizes that they have valuable experience and knowledge. A fundamental goal of most mentoring programmes is to help prepare future managers, so that young employees understand the demanding nature of an executive position and can make the transition from junior to senior management more easily.

By the same token, the mentor must have skills that are currently valuable to pass on. No matter how empathetic he may be, the plateaued manager who has been put out to grass and whose knowledge of the company's inner councils is obsolete, will be a poor mentor.

It is useful if a mentor and protégé share similar work experiences so that they can better identify with each other. It is unlikely that a mentor in accounts will be as useful to the protégé in personnel, as the mentor who is in staff management. If they are in the same or complementary areas of work it is more likely that the mentor will understand his protégé's difficulties and will be able to supply him with advice and solutions drawn from similar personal experience.

The mentor who encourages and motivates

The ability to encourage and motivate is another important interpersonal skill that the mentor must have in abundance if the relationship with his protégé is to reach its full potential.

The mentor must be able to recognize the ability of his protégé and make it clear to him that he believes in his capacity to progress within the company. He must be willing to let the protégé rely on him for as long as he needs to, as well as be willing to help him to become independent eventually.

The mentor encourages the protégé through recognizing the different roles he can play. For a certain period he can be a reassuring parental figure to whom the protégé can turn for support and sympathy. The mentor must also at this stage be willing to let his protégé identify with him and use him as a role model. At other stages of the relationship, the mentor can encourage his protégé to become more independent and start to make individual decisions.

One mentor in a Civil Service department recalls how difficult it was to learn this lesson:

> I had this intelligent individual who was highly motivated. I expected his progress to be extremely rapid, but was surprised to find that he seemed to depend on me for quite some time. I was worried about it and considered whether I ought to try to force him somehow to make his own decisions unaided by me. Eventually I decided to go at his pace and not the pace I expected. He is now at a higher level than me in the company, but recently came to me to thank me for not rushing him in that first year. He explained he had found it very difficult to adjust to his new job and had found the new pressure especially hard to cope with. Apparently, my support and encouragement had kept him going through it all.

The ability to encourage and motivate is an especially important skill for the mentor if, as we discussed in chapter 4, the company has a deliberate policy of not promoting high-flyers until they have a broad base of experience. If these people are to be prevented from seeking faster promotion elsewhere, the mentor has to help them extract a high degree of job satisfaction from their experiences now and let them know they will reap the rewards for their patience later in their career.

One corporate mentor explains:

We get so many MBAs coming straight from college who expect to race up the promotion ladder. Without a mentor to explain the system to them, few of them realize that this is just not the way we operate. If we discover a talented individual, we allocate him to different areas of the company before we promote him so that he understands and has been directly involved in all aspects of the business.

A young manager in a small British defence firm emphasizes the point with reference to the difference the support of a senior manager made to his career.

I graduated with an engineering degree and immediately took my MBA. I then successfully applied for the position of technical manager, which had just been newly created in a defence firm. I found my new job extremely difficult because I was dealing with engineers who were obviously far more experienced than I and whose technical knowledge far outmatched mine. They plainly resented my presence. A few were even openly hostile to me.

Fortunately, since my position was new to the company itself, a senior manager had been asked to help me as much as possible. He supported and encouraged me. Sometimes it was only this which stopped me from leaving. More importantly he helped me to recognize that my difficulties were not caused by my own incompetence or failure, as I had originally thought, but that in fact the engineers' hostility had another cause and was aimed at my position rather than at me personally. He explained that the company had been trying to get the structure of the technical side of the company more into line with central management. I was just unlucky to be caught in the middle of a war between management and the engineers.

Armed with the knowledge that he was fully supported by top management, this young manager was able to ride the storm until he won the respect of the engineering staff.

The mentor who nurtures

The mentor must be able to create an open, candid atmosphere which will encourage the protégé to confide in and trust him. The mentor is there to draw out the protégé and help him to discover his identity within the corporation. With the help of the mentor the protégé assesses himself and discovers where his skills, aspirations and interests lie. Most importantly, the mentor must be able to listen to his protégé and ask open-ended questions that will draw the younger person out. If necessary, the company should consider giving mentors training in both listening and interviewing skills.

One key test of the mentor who nurtures is his track record of bringing along subordinates. If his department has provided a consistent breeding ground for talented young supervisors and managers, then the chances are high that he will make a good mentor for people from other departments.

The mentor who teaches

This is a skill which the mentor himself may need to be taught, because being a really good teacher does not come naturally to many people. Highly ambitious, self-motivated people (and the description applies to most people who make it to top management) often lack the patience to teach. Yet the mentor must know how to maximize his protégé's opportunities to learn. He does this by creating a stimulating environment which consistently challenges the protégé to apply theory to the real world of management.

A mentor may teach his protégé through:

(a) Holding 'what if?' sessions where he guides the protégé in problem-solving discussions to encourage him to discover as many alternatives as possible.

(b) Discussing with the protégé real problems the mentor is currently dealing with or has recently dealt with. Rather than expand upon the cleverness of his own solutions, the mentor asks the protégé what course of action he would take. The mentor can often complete the analysis by telling the protégé the solutions he actually devised and why he chose them. In this way, through mini internal case studies, he gives the protégé an insight into decision-making in higher level jobs.

(c) Playing devil's advocate. In the protective environment of his office, the mentor teaches the protégé how to assert his opinions and influence his listener under difficult situations. The mentor plays aggressive and threatening roles so that the protégé learns to handle stressful and potentially explosive situations. A vice-chairman in an advertising company was helped in his career by a senior executive in the corporation. This mentor invited opposition from his protégé and frequently acted in a domineering and brusque manner. The mentor's aim was to help develop in his protégé an aggressiveness that he considered was essential for success in that field. The vice-chairman comments:

> Before I met my mentor I was not particularly forceful. However, when I talked to him I found I had the choice either to be chewed up, or to assert myself. He constantly pushed me in these one-to-one confrontations so that now when I talk to a client I have developed a way of expressing my opinions with weight and force.

(d) Working on a project with the protégé and displaying the management skills and styles necessary to get the job done. At AMI Healthcare this is seen as one of the mentor's top priorities.

Using a variety of techniques, the mentor creates a continuous learning environment for the protégé.

In the North West region of ICI's engineering department, for example, the mentor is expected to:

- probe to help the protégé learn more about experiences and their significance
- challenge the conclusions the protégé has reached
- check and validate technical and non-technical content
- open up other avenues of enquiry
- direct the protégé towards reading material which may give perspective or provide depth.

Merril Lynch's mentors have run a variety of special activities for their protégés, including:

1 visits to important business centres such as the New York Stock Exchange, as well as to regional offices of the company
2 arranging discussions on useful topics such as planning, budgeting, how to network and the structure of the firm
3 allocating the responsibility of organizing meetings to protégés. A mentor helps the protégé to develop communication skills by arranging for him to give a talk, use slides and write reports for the programme newsletter.

Many mentors commented on how rewarding they found the experience and how they felt they learnt personally from the programme. Comments included: 'It helped me to realize how important it is to develop staff' and 'It put me more in touch with the company and helped me understand better the difficulties which young managers face.'

The mentor who offers mutual respect

The most essential ingredient in any mentoring relationship is mutual respect between the two partners. If the protégé does not respect and trust his mentor's opinion, advice and influence, the benefits from the relationship will be severely limited. Programme co-ordinators must remember that a protégé's attitude towards the mentor will inevitably be influenced by the mentor's general reputation within the company.
 To be more precise, the protégé will:

(a) Assess the mentor's professional reputation by scrutinizing his past performance. If a mentor has been involved with too many failed projects the protégé is likely to feel that a close alliance with that person will do his career little good.
(b) Assess the mentor's interpersonal skills. For example, a protégé may feel that a rewarding relationship could not be established with a mentor who is heard of only through memos and telephone calls.
(c) Assess the mentor's status with his colleagues. If the mentor commands respect and esteem from his peers, the protégé

feels his career will benefit from being associated with him.

(d) Assess the mentor's corporate alliances. The protégé must believe that his mentor has enough power in the organization to make a tangible difference to his career.

The mentor who responds

The good mentor will be action-oriented. In other words, he will not be merely a passive listener, but will react to issues and problems the protégé brings him, by providing practical help. He will, for example, make introductions and open doors. He will also intervene when he sees the protégé heading in a dangerous direction, if only to prevent the protégé damaging the mentor's own network of relationships.

Checklist: ideal characteristics to seek in a mentor

Look for a manager who:

1 already has a good record for developing other people
2 has a genuine interest in seeing younger people advance and can relate to their problems
3 has a wide range of current skills to pass on
4 has a good understanding of the organization, how it works and where it is going
5 combines patience with good interpersonal skills and an ability to work in an unstructured programme
6 has sufficient time to devote to the relationship
7 can command a protégé's respect
8 has his own network of contacts and influence.

Checklist: characteristics to avoid in a mentor

1 Try not to appoint as a mentor someone who is heavily engaged in corporate politics. The protégé could easily become a pawn in a power game between senior executives.
2 Do not assign a protégé to a mentor who has been appointed

recently to a new position. He will still be working himself into the job and will not have enough time for the protégé. He will also need time to establish his own status with his new peers before he can promote the protégé. This mentor's informal network system would not be developed enough at this stage either.

3   Make sure that a protégé is not allocated to a mentor who is involved in activities which carry little weight in the company. If the company is more orientated towards marketing than finance, the protégé will feel he has been placed on the side-lines of power if his mentor specializes in accounting. The protégé must feel his mentor represents a direct line to promotion.

4   Do not choose a mentor who is obviously on the way down in the company. The protégé will fear constantly that the mentor will take him with him.

5   Do not choose someone with a consistently high turnover of staff to be a mentor. Closely examine the mentor's department and assess how high staff morale is there.

Selecting mentors: practical examples

The NHS General Management Training Scheme in Wales requires mentors to be accredited by the Manpower Consultancy Service. Accreditation is based on past experience and current skills levels. The NHS sees its mentors as having to fulfil five major roles:

Coach – teaches the protégé to analyse work experience
Co-ordinator – ensures input from others is incorporated into the training
Supporter – helps in the transition from university to business life
Monitor – an essential link in the examination process
Organizer – responsible for allocating a protégé to an NHS district.

To take part in the NHS scheme, a mentor needs to:

• show evidence of commitment to management development

- understand and be committed to NHS general management
- be in a post of sufficient seniority
- be perceived by the trainee as approachable
- have coaching and counselling skills
- have vision to help the trainee develop
- have the support of his/her senior officer
- be willing to participate in training activities
- be able to give sufficient time to the trainee.

A Trafalgar House Construction Holding spokesman says:

> The choice of mentor is made between the protégé, his boss and the managing director. In some cases, the managing director has overruled the protégé's first choice, either because he feels the mentor is likely to benefit him more politically than developmentally, or because he is aware of changes that will make another senior manager more suitable for the role.

Advice to the mentor

1   Do not assume that your protégé feels satisfied with the relationship just because you are. Make sure that you provide the protégé with some opportunity to discuss openly any criticisms he may have about your methods and behaviour.
2   Ensure that your protégé is not intimidated or over-influenced by your personality. Remember that your aim is not to produce a clone of yourself. Try to discover how he responds to you by putting your influence to the test. Note how often your protégé speaks when you are near. Has your protégé adopted any of your mannerisms? When you put forward an opinion which is obviously incorrect, does your protégé differ or agree?
3   Avoid confining your protégé's growth potential to your limitations. Ask yourself if you are willing to allow your protégé possibly to outstrip you in his career.

The mentor's view

Executive mentors at Trafalgar House Construction take a wide range of views about the roles they play and the characteristics they need to present. Among their comments:

> 'It's Catch-22 . . . The more able mentors are people who are lateral thinkers. The people who stand to gain most, however, are those who started off with blinkers on.'

> 'The mentor has to make sure he sees his man frequently enough. That's difficult to define. You can't say it's once a month, once a week, or once every six months, because the course changes . . . but it's important for the mentor to take an active role in saying "What are you doing? Let's sit down and talk." . . . It's up to the mentor to make the running and make sure the guy is on the straight and level.'

> 'It's nice to be able to talk about something which isn't "Are we going to make any money" or "How can we avoid losing money?" It's a different thought process you go through.'

> 'If I heard second hand that any I was involved with as a mentor had a problem, I'd feel I hadn't been doing my job of mentoring very well.'

> 'I've reached a stage of life now, where a prime motive for me is getting people who'll fill in the slots – including my slot eventually.'

> 'Don't take it on if you feel it is the done thing, if people are asking you because there's no other willing horse. Take it on with the view that you are going to profit by it.'

Summary

Selecting the mentor is a critical task. Good mentors have empathy, experience and excellence. They must act as surrogate parents, combining authority and friendship, counsel and commitment.

Chapter 6
Choosing the protégé

The criteria for choosing protégés, like those for mentors, will vary from company to company and from industry to industry, according to the qualities and skills the company identifies as being essential to management in their corporate culture.

Especially where the programme is specifically aimed at high-flyers, mentoring gives the company a chance, if it wishes to take it, to break the existing leadership mould and prime itself with a generation of future senior managers more fitted to the company's projected needs 10 years ahead. Informal godfather relationships tend to form around a senior manager's recognition of his younger self in a junior manager. This is a process which tends to perpetuate a cycle of people of similar types and it can be dangerous when the demands of the top management job require individuals with different characteristics. Either the company fails to achieve the quality of leadership it needs, or it is forced to bring in senior management from outside, which is in itself a risky business.

In implementing a formal mentoring programme, companies have an unusual opportunity to reassess the essential qualities of leadership they need for the future and to cultivate a new generation of managers who exhibit that range of abilities.

Before deciding the selection criteria, an organization must first clarify which particular group of employees it is orientating the programme towards. For example, is the mentoring programme catering for:

(a) high-flyers? Is the mentoring programme serving as a fast avenue to promotion for those employees with ability and strong potential for future leadership?

(b) underrepresented groups, such as women and ethnic minorities? Is the programme an instrument of positive discrimination, basing its selection primarily on gender and race?
(c) managers in general? Are the programme co-ordinators attempting to improve the quality of performance of all professional, supervisory and management employees, regardless of individual competence or future potential?

Selection criteria

Once the organization has decided the orientation of the programme, it will be able to plan its selection procedure.

Stringent and carefully thought out selection criteria may make all the difference to the success or failure of a mentoring programme. Poor selection may demotivate the protégé's peers, who may have been passed over for someone they believe to be of lesser ability. It will waste senior management time (often the scarcest and most valuable resource the company has) and it may undermine the whole mentoring programme by bringing it into dispute.

At Security Pacific National Bank Inc in California, vice-president of personnel, Bennett Dolin, explains how his company learnt the importance of selecting protégés carefully. 'Where we had failures, the main reason was poor selection. Some people looked a lot better than they were. As they went through the programme, we realized they had no substance to match the appearance.' Dolin's company now carefully screens each applicant.

At National Westminster Bank, the mentoring programme encourages potential high-flyers to move onto the fast track at an early stage. Interested candidates undergo a series of rigorous tests and interviews. If they are deemed to have potential, they then attend a week-long training course where their potential is discussed and they are given practical suggestions for personal development.

The selection process varies widely. For example, Marks and Spencer has used mentoring at various levels, especially for new recruits and senior managers working towards executive level. The company allows mentors to vote for their protégés, and protégés state which mentor they would prefer.

The company then tries to match the requests.

Each of the fourteen companies in Trafalgar House Construction Holdings can nominate up to three candidates for the programme each year. These managers must have been in the company for at least two years. Up to fourteen are chosen annually.

At Merrill Lynch, the protégé's immediate supervisor nominates a pool of candidates and completes recommendation reports for each. The company feels that the protégé's manager knows far more about the young person's day-to-day behaviour and ability than the programme co-ordinators. The intention is to base selection upon solid track record rather than on the protégé's ability to promote himself at one-off interviews.

The manager also lists the protégé's:

(a) major strengths and weaknesses of personality and professional ability
(b) developmental needs in order to assist the programme co-ordinators in judging whether mentoring will be useful to the protégé
(c) current performance, especially detailing any notably demanding projects the protégé has been involved in
(d) potential for advancement and ability to take greater responsibility.

Merrill Lynch also gives potential protégés application forms. The applicants state:

(a) why they think they are suitable candidates
(b) what benefits and skills they wish to obtain from the programme
(c) what kind of self development activities they have pursued in the past year.

The Chicago-based retailer, Jewel Companies, runs a mentoring programme for employees who are highly likely to advance to senior management. The qualities which selectors look for in protégés are strong interpersonal skills. If the protégé is destined to become a company leader it is essential that he should be able to communicate diplomatically and effectively. He must be able to work well with colleagues, interact easily with clients and maintain the support and liking of subordinates. AMI Healthcare selects its protégés on current performance and on potential for enriching their role within the organization.

Elizabeth Alleman, of Leadership Development Inc (Akron, USA), describes the qualities which she believes are important in a protégé:

> Primarily, the protégé should be selected on the basis of talent and potential. However, almost as important, he must demonstrate an eagerness to learn and a willingness to spend extra time and energy on the programme.

Security Pacific National Bank runs two mentoring programmes. The first was implemented in 1977 in order to improve the career opportunities of women and ethnic minorities. Since the entry to the programme was not solely based on performance and potential the firm did not devise stringent selective methods. Instead, it gave its senior executives the responsibility of picking a suitable candidate and grooming that person for an executive position. Since the programme started, nearly 500 protégés have been promoted to senior positions.

The second mentoring programme run by Security Pacific is the Advanced Opportunities Programme, which is a follow-up to the first. Selection processes are stricter since its aim is to prepare high-potential employees for senior management positions quickly and effectively. Department heads nominate their own employees, based on:

(a) current performance ratings
(b) the protégé's demonstrated interest in self development
(c) the protégé's ability to assume a senior position within two, to two and a half years.

Nominations are passed to executive vice-presidents who make the final selections, as well as assigning the protégé to a mentor.

Charlotte Shelton, researching mentoring for the First National Bank, describes the qualities of an effective protégé who is likely to be highly receptive to a mentor. A protégé needs to have eight important traits. He must be:

positive minded
able to show insight and sensitivity
flexible
self aware
non defensive
conscientious and well organized
able to laugh at mistakes
a fast learner.

Author Michael Zey also attempts to identify the qualities in a protégé which are most likely to attract a mentor.

1 Intelligence

The junior manager must be able to identify and solve business problems rapidly.

2 Ambition

The protégé must be gifted and have the ambition to channel his ability into career advancement. The mentor also wants to further his career and looks for a protégé who will advance through the organization with him.

3 Succession potential

The mentor also wants a protégé who demonstrates that he is capable of performing the mentor's own job. The mentor wants to be sure that he has groomed a replacement.

4 Strong interpersonal skills

The protégé must be able to make new alliances for the mentor as well as retaining the ones the mentor has already established.

A study carried out in the United States in 1982 adds a further important, if somewhat obvious, characteristic. It found that employees who performed visible, risky and important tasks were three times as likely to form mentoring relationships of their own accord as those who took few risks. It suggests that mentor relationships succeed and are more mutually rewarding if the protégé is chosen for his general, all-round reputation for hard work, enthusiasm and ability.

Must the protégé share the same qualities as his mentor?

There is a common assertion that in order for a mentoring relationship to succeed, the protégé must have a similar personality to the mentor. Elizabeth Alleman and her colleague Isadore Newman attempted to establish if a similarity of personality or background was indeed the basis of rewarding mentor relationships. Alleman and Newman studied 100 managers, 29 pairs reporting a mentoring relationship and 21 pairs reporting a typical business relationship. The two compared the relationship between the mentor and the protégé to the relationship between a manager and his superior. Through using personality tests and questionnaires they discovered:

(a) Mentoring pairs have no more similarities in personality or background than non-mentored pairs. When participants described themselves and their partners, their profiles contained few shared traits.
(b) Mentoring relationships are not based on complementary personality traits. Newman and Alleman did not find evidence to support the suggestion that mentors choose protégés whose strengths and skills offset the mentor's weaknesses.
(c) Mentors do not believe there are any special similarities between themselves and their protégés.
(d) Protégés view their mentors as similar to ideal workers and identify with them to a greater extent than managers who have a non-mentoring relationship with their supervisor.

In short, Alleman and Newman demonstrate that it is not essential for the mentor and protégé to have similar personalities or backgrounds. Indeed, as we have seen, if a cultural readjustment is needed in the organization, then it may pay to avoid deliberately too close a match.

Summary

Mentoring is a disciplined process, although it has few rules. The organization should decide and explain carefully who it wants to mentor and why, the criteria for selection, and who will do the selecting. The criteria will vary from company to company but should always be drawn against the background of this question: 'How much will this person gain from a mentoring relationship?'

Chapter 7
Setting up the mentoring programme

Some form of spontaneous mentoring takes place in most organizations, whether acknowledged or not. A formalized programme helps harness it to the organization's objectives. Properly managed, the programme can enhance the benefits to individuals from informal mentoring and minimize the problems that arise when the informal system bypasses talented employees.

There are usually four people involved in a mentoring programme. Together, they make up a mentoring quadrangle:

- the protégé
- the mentor
- the line manager
- the trainer, who monitors the relationship and looks at resources for training opportunities.

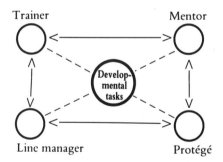

The clearer all four are about the objectives and effort required, the more successful the programme will be. All must be involved and consulted about career moves and developmental tasks that will take the protégé away from day-to-day work and responsibilities.

Each organization has to draw up a mentoring programme

that fits its particular company culture and answers the needs of its own employees. To ensure the success of the mentoring programme, a company must be prepared to be flexible in its approach and be willing to assess continuously and, if necessary, modify the methods it has implemented. Although this book focuses on relatively disciplined programmes, an increasing number of organizations – particularly fast-growing medium-sized companies or institutions facing rapid cultural change – are opting for programmes with a much more informal approach. For example, they may train a number of mentors, then allow them to select their own protégés, within broad guidelines.

The starting point, as with any major corporate programme, must be a clear statement of objectives, against which progress may be measured. Typical objectives might be:

1   to establish a cadre of broadly trained generalist managers at or just below middle management
2   to speed and improve the induction of specific types of recruits and reduce wastage within the first year of their employment
3   to allow top management to assess the ability of both individual young managers and the rising generation of managers as a whole
4   to provide equal opportunities for disadvantaged groups of employees.

In each case, the personnel department can establish with top management a set of assessment criteria and a timetable for achieving specific levels of results.

Putting these objectives into practice requires a great deal of preparation. Usually at least six months to a year is needed to gain acceptance of the concept from the key people in the organization, to establish objectives and measurements, to design supporting facilities, such as special training courses, and to begin the process of selecting participants.

Before setting up its mentoring programme, for example, the Burton Group's human resources department decided to look at the following:

• the internal set-up and relationships

- support systems
- timescales to be agreed
- obtaining the managing directors' commitment
- determining how it would select mentors
- how it would prepare mentoring workshops
- how to match the mentor and protégé
- introducing the mentor and the protégé
- the line manager's role.

Throughout this process, the following principles are essential to bear in mind:

ensure top management commitment
adapt the programme to the company's development programme
ensure commitment and participation
ensure an acceptance of the time involved
match the mentor and protégé carefully
demystify the mentoring programme.

Preparing the company for a mentoring programme

1 Ensure top management commitment

Ensure that top management is committed to the programme. The top management team needs to supply decisive leadership to demonstrate to the rest of the company that it considers mentoring to be a legitimate and effective method of developing and improving staff potential. Top management must support the programme verbally and materially. It must promote mentoring within the company, through speeches, letters, memoranda and articles in the company newspaper. Articles in the public media can reinforce the message greatly, because employees often take greater note of information they read in independent newspapers and magazines than they do of the same information presented in official company publications. Senior management can also attend general meetings of groups of mentoring pairs. These strategies are especially necessary if general unease, confusion, or even suspicion about the programme exists in the company.

2 Adapt the programme to the company's development programme

Try to fit the mentoring programme into the context of a wider framework of employee development and human resource management, and explain this framework to employees. Problems are likely to arise if the programme exists in isolation. If it seems that mentoring is the only form of career development in the company, employees may easily assume that those chosen to participate are destined automatically for senior management. The company could be accused of having a promotion system based solely on favouritism. The morale of those not on the programme would suffer appreciably. Those individuals who are on the programme may be encouraged to believe that all their chances of promotion lie in the mentoring relationship. As a result, they may throw all their efforts into that area and neglect other aspects of their work. To avoid these pitfalls, mentoring should be seen as only one dimension of career development.

The company should also make sure protégés have other opportunities to improve their skills beyond those arising within the mentoring programme. They should have access to internal or external workshops, self-development and distance-learning materials, as well as career development classes. This is to ensure that protégés can easily supplement their knowledge if the mentor's coaching is too specialized or fails to be sufficiently relevant and helpful. If the protégé is forced to rely solely on an inefficient mentor, he can feel frustrated and limited by the relationship. For female protégés in particular, the company should also consider the applicability of assertiveness training.

3 Ensure commitment and participation

Ensure that participation is voluntary. Mentoring demands time and effort so the essential ingredient is commitment. When a company requests staff to volunteer to be mentors, it should make sure that it emphasizes how demanding the relationship is. The career development co-ordinator should talk to all mentor applicants before making the final decision. If an assessment centre approach is used to select protégés, consideration should be given to designing an assessment centre for mentors, too.

Potential mentors should be informed of problems and

challenges, and what they should expect of the relationship. AMI Healthcare, for example, now gives all its new mentors the chance to hear from existing mentors of the pitfalls and pleasures mentoring can bring. The career development co-ordinator should also attempt to discover any ambivalence the mentor may feel about his commitment.

4 Ensure support systems are in place

Pilkington Glass appoints an Administrative Co-ordinator – like the Prudential's 'Supermentor' – who oversees all the mentors. The Administrative Co-ordinator also identifies potential mentors based on their commitment to developing individuals, experience and accessibility. He ensures they are properly trained and then explains and monitors the mentoring relationship. Pilkington also appoints Functional Facilitators, who are experienced specialists. They ensure the mentor has the appropriate experience and insight before the relationship starts. They can also identify opportunities for the protégé that the mentor may have missed. All those supporting the mentor and protégé are responsible for the success of the relationship and meet regularly to discuss it.

5 Ensure an acceptance of the time involved

Make sure everyone understands the amount of time commitment involved. As part of the preparation of the mentor, the protégé and the protégé's boss must be devoted to establishing just how much of each person's time will be taken up by the scheme. This time has to be planned for, regular meetings scheduled and a timetable established for any project work agreed.

Two key questions that must be asked are:

— How disruptive to the normal work of these people will the time commitment be?
— How valuable will this time and effort be in achieving the objective of developing the protégé?

One useful suggestion is that the mentoring pair contract at first for a six month trial, during which time they can get to know one another. At the end of this period the arrangement can be continued as needed, or gradually dissolved, with no offence to either party.

6 Match the mentor and protégé carefully

Choose and match both the mentor and the protégé carefully. Where the protégé is concerned, some formal mentoring programmes use a nominating procedure. Managers in each department suggest those individuals whom they feel would be suitable. This decision would be based upon:

(a) how committed the protégé is likely to be
(b) how able the protégé is
(c) how receptive he would be in a relationship where he would defer to the mentor's greater knowledge and experience. Some young managers may dislike this subordinate position
(d) how much the protégé would benefit overall from this form of career development. Some individuals, for example the real loner, may respond better to a more conventional career programme.

When matching mentors and protégés the Burton Group looks at:

- personalities
- experience
- breadth of knowledge
- qualificational background
- status.

The NHS in Wales allows its mentors to bid for protégés. This choice then has to be approved.

Some companies also select mentors by nominations from their peers. Part of the reasoning here is that the middle manager's colleagues are more likely to have a sound knowledge of his management abilities and interpersonal skills than either the co-ordinators of the programme or the board. When AMI Healthcare first began mentoring, it matched protégés' weaknesses with mentor's strengths, but personality clashes proved troublesome. When it began its second programme, protégés were invited to choose their own mentors, naming a first and second choice and stating what they hoped to get out of the relationship. However, this time some mentors were chosen by too many protégés. The protégés often found it hard to make a second choice, because they had little idea of the skills and experience available. On the third programme, managers were asked if they wanted a mentor at all (all seemed to) and then asked to choose one, citing their reasons. Typical responses included: 'I respect his management style, and communications skills and have in the past found his advice useful'; 'She clearly has an overall understanding of AMI systems and the running of hospitals, and I am impressed by the knowledge she has of the company, management and operational skills and her commitment and enthusiasm.'

7 Demystify the mentoring programme

Demystify the mentoring programme for those who are uninvolved. The methods and objectives of the programme should be explained clearly, setting out and emphasizing the benefits to the organization as a whole. If it is possible to establish only a small number of mentoring pairs at the beginning of a programme, the organization should explain to failed applicants that they will have an opportunity to reapply in the future.

8 Ensure confidentiality

Confidentiality is essential if the protégé is to open up to the mentor to produce the kind of frank relationship necessary for success. BP Chemicals ensures all exchanges are covered by a rule of confidentiality, so that the protégé can speak to the mentor as a trusted friend. One mentor comments: 'The mentor should be completely aside from the line of work. It is important that total honesty and openness can be displayed, and often protégés feel wary if they do not have the distance they would like.'

The NW region of ICI's engineering department feels there are occasions when the mentor may run into personal conflict between perceived loyalty to the charge versus loyalty to the company. This may be brought into focus when the six-month report is prepared. The written report asks the mentor to comment on technical competence; people skills; motivation; potential; future career directions. It provides information which is of use to the company and some mentors feel it may compromise their position of trust with the charge. The counter-argument would be that it is important for mentor and charge to have an open relationship and that must inevitably include a discussion of career choice in its widest context. The company expects the six monthly report to be crisp but not to break confidentiality.

How to prepare the mentor and the protégé

It is essential to supply as much information as possible to the two most important participants of the programme: the mentor and the protégé, for both need to understand the purpose and objectives of the programme for the individual and for the company. The advantages of the relationship to both the mentor and the protégé should be particularly emphasized.

1 The mentor

The most important aim in the preparatory stage of the programme is to motivate the mentor and help him to recognize how he can contribute to the protégé's development.
    An organization can:

(a) Run workshops for the mentor suggesting various teaching methods. A series of seven sessions might deal with:

   — the benefits of the mentoring relationship
   — the dynamic nature of the relationship, its stages and phases
   — ways to increase the protégé's competence
   — ways to increase the protégé's self esteem
   — ways to help the protégé to get ahead
   — anticipating and forestalling possible problems
   — adapting mentoring practices to particular settings.

These workshops could operate through brainstorming sessions as well as role play and critique sessions so that mentors can assist each other to develop greater skills. These sessions would also encourage mentors to act as a support network for each other. Typically, in the UK, the mentor training workshops last 1–2 days and focus both on building awareness of the role and on honing key mentoring skills such as coaching and career counselling.

For example, having run a mentoring scheme for several years, Pilkington Glass now sends all managers on the training programme 'How to be an effective mentor'. Not all instantly go on to become mentors, but the training is seen as worthwhile for all managers. Similarly, BP Chemical's mentors take part in a one-day training session which outlines the purpose of mentoring and the counselling techniques needed to make it a success.

Most of the successful schemes follow the training route. However, the 1989 Industrial Society/ITEM survey, 'The Line Manager as Developer of Talent', found that a high proportion gave mentors no training support.

(b) Provide the mentor with a frame of reference so that he can evaluate how his mentoring relationship is progressing. For example, a schedule showing issues he should cover with the protégé over the first six months of the relationship will help to focus on specific activities. Demonstrate how he can set the protégé demanding tasks such as presentation talks to senior management. A new mentor often takes time to learn how best to approach the relationship. The reassurance of firm guidelines will be useful initially and can be modified later as he grows in confidence and expertise. Again, Pilkington gives each mentor a mentoring pack which helps him to train on an ongoing basis. It acts as a communication channel and information is constantly updated as the relationship develops. The pack contains lists of other mentors, training material, experiences of the appraisal scheme and so on.

Training sessions must confront specific questions such as:

How can the mentor provide greater visibility for his protégé this week?
To whom should he promote the protégé?

How can he improve a weak area of the protégé's knowledge?
How much time should he spend with his protégé?

However, try to avoid making the model too rigid or you will constrain the mentor from following up the protégé's *ad hoc* needs: minimize the rules and maximize the personal freedom of the mentor. Encouragement should be given to build his mentoring strategies around his own management style, so that he feels as comfortable as possible in his mentoring role. Flexibility is the most suitable and rewarding approach to this type of relationship.

(c) Help the mentor to examine frankly the potential risks involved in being a mentor. Programme co-ordinators should make it clear to the mentor and the company in general that the relationship is not guaranteed to be successful and that a failed pairing will not reflect badly on the mentor. AMI Healthcare sees one of the major roles of its HR department as to stress to the mentor that if the mentoring relationship breaks down it will not be deemed a 'failure'. Since the project is initiated and co-ordinated by upper management, responsibility for its success clearly lies with the company and not with the individual.

(d) Alert 'cross-gender' mentors to the potential problems. The discovery that rumour and sexual innuendo exists about a mentoring couple can decisively restrict or even destroy the relationship. If the two parties are forewarned they can cope with the external pressures better, or adopt strategies to avoid giving encouragement to rumour.

(e) Introduce the mentor to other managers who have experience in mentorship and who can discuss the various stages of the relationship and the challenges and difficulties which are likely to arise. The NW region of ICI's engineering department arranges for mentors to meet periodically as a group so they can exchange news, compare standards and approaches and discuss problems they have faced. A spokesman commented: 'The job can be a lonely one and informal discussions can help keep the checks and balances in perspective. This is important because our mentors are widely dispersed across about fifteen locations.' In the same way, a speaker who has had a mentor himself can be an invaluable source of information for new mentors on such issues as how the protégé views the mentor as he moves from dependence to independence and autonomy.

(f) Appoint a senior or 'super' mentor to counsel and guide the less experienced mentors.

A useful summary comes from the US Bureau of Business Practice 'Management Letter', which suggests all mentors should be advised of the following:

- Choose a protégé you can identify with
- Clearly define the relationship at the outset
- Act as a sponsor for your protégé
- Coach your protégé in diagnosing and resolving problems: 'The worst possible thing to do is tell a protégé what to do. Instead, help diagnose what the causes are; if that's done well, the solution will be obvious,' says Dr Warner Burke, Professor of Psychology, Columbia University
- Help your protégé learn from mistakes: 'The mentor's role is to make sure that the protégé learns from mistakes because the biggest way to fail is to make the same mistake twice. And people won't do that if they learn from the first,' says Dr Burke
- Observe your protégé in action in order to pinpoint strengths and weaknesses and give him or her feedback on those
- Coach your protégé in making critical decisions in terms of career paths and in developing the skills necessary to attain career goals. The protégé should always have someone to go to when taking a career decision
- Recognize the benefits mentoring offers you. As one mentor commented: 'I hear a lot and learn a lot. People tell me about how they view what's happening down in the troops in other areas of the organization, so I get a good perspective on what's going on. In many instances I have learned about something through the mentoring process that has helped me do my job better. Mentoring helps me stay current.'

2 The protégé

To ensure protégés extract the most from a mentoring

programme they can also attend preliminary meetings. They can:

(a) Study the organization of the company, the relationship between departments and the career structure. Protégés need to understand how the real career routes work. Formal promotion routes, which are identified in induction materials, may not be quite so simple as they seem. Other factors come into play. For example, many multinational companies expect a manager to have international experience before he can proceed above a certain level. Just as what stage he obtains that experience can make a strong difference to his promotion prospects. If too early, it may be felt he did not have the ability at that time to learn enough. If too late, it may take him away from head office just when the maximum opportunities are likely to occur.

In other companies, the official policy may state that there are equal career opportunities. Yet in reality the company culture may, for example, give preference to people in certain disciplines, such as sales over production or accounts. The protégé must recognize how the mentor can help him through this maze of alternatives, in order to find his own 'fast track.'

(b) Spend time on self assessment and identify personal strengths and weaknesses, which the protégé can then improve through mentoring.

(c) Clarify personal career aspirations, both in terms of vertical and horizontal movement.

(d) Construct action plans, for both the long term and the short term. When the protégé meets with his mentor he then has a clear starting point for discussion.

(e) Pilkington Glass also gives its protégés a mentoring pack so the mentor doesn't have to spend excessive time going over the basics of the relationship.

Bringing the mentor and protégé together

Ensure that the mentor and the protégé have a preliminary meeting where they can discuss the expectations each partner holds. One of the potential pitfalls of a formalized programme is that the protégé wants and expects more than is possible from the mentor. The role and responsibility of each must be fully clarified. At the beginning of the programme the expectations of each should be fairly modest so that there is room for negotiation when they review the relationship at a later period. At that point, if the relationship has been successful the mentor and protégé can decide to strengthen their commitment to each other. If it has failed, they can terminate the relationship on good terms, without the protégé feeling disappointed because his expectations turned out to be unrealistic.

AMI Healthcare mentors are paired with protégés about four weeks prior to the programme and are encouraged to meet informally as soon as possible. Protégés and mentors are brought together collectively on the first day of the programme and then meet in private in the evening to discuss what they want to achieve from the relationship. This is then discussed with the group and the Human Resources department, which can monitor and stimulate.

The NHS in Wales holds an informal meeting for mentors and protégés to assess chemistry and allow them to swop views. Each protégé is assessed as to development needs, mobility, domestic commitments and so on. The pairs then visit their placement hospitals before the scheme starts, to help build trust between the two and to resolve practical problems.

Include the protégé's immediate superior

The mentor should ensure that the protégé's boss is involved in the programme and is kept informed about all activities. If the line manager supports rather than opposes the programme, he can participate effectively in creating suitable opportunities for the protégé to learn and can reconcile the protégé's need for development with the day-to-day demands of the job. It is a good idea if the protégé, his manager and the mentor meet before the start of the programme to decide when the protégé does work assigned by his mentor and when he does his normal tasks. They should also discuss the possibility of conflicting interests and loyalties arising. The mentor and the protégé's manager should construct clear lines of communication, possibly meeting regularly, so that if problems do arise they can solve them quickly and easily. Bass Brewing makes sure mentors have regular discussions with line managers about the younger person. The mentor clears uses of the protégé's time with the line manager, who is seen to share the development responsibility.

The protégé's manager should also be kept informed about what the objectives of the mentoring relationship are. If kept in ignorance, the manager may suspect the mentor's career guidance includes how the protégé can obtain his job. It is the responsibility both of the mentor and the protégé to keep the manager involved, to ensure that he is an ally rather than an adversary. At Pilkington Glass, the line manager carries out the protégé's six-month appraisal. This ensures the mentor does not break confidentiality and, while the mentor is *consulted*, the line manager feels (and is) in control of the appraisal activity. He also produces a plan of the protégé's tasks and responsibilities to give to the mentor.

Testing the programme

Start in a modest way to make sure that the initial effort is well designed and fulfils its objectives. Once a trial programme, involving say four or five mentoring pairs, has been successfully established, the company can decide to be more ambitious and expand its size and time scale. In this way the organization can avoid most of the disillusionment and backlash that can come when a full-blown programme fails to live up to its objectives.

The role of the training department

Just how far the training department does and should become involved varies from organization to organization. At British Gas, for example, four-way communication between the different points of the mentoring quadrangle is emphasized, although, according to one of their Recruitment and Development Reports:

> Line managers are expected to liaise with mentors, rather than with the training department, although the training

department does provide a 'safety net' for mentoring relationships that go wrong.

A major role of the training department is communication. The department has recently published guidelines, for example, making clear in advance to mentors and line managers the kind of time commitment graduates need to give to the graduate programme and specific development projects. The company's electronic mail network allows the training department to communicate frequently with both mentors and graduates.

At the opposite extreme, other companies take a more relaxed approach, where the training department delivers initial training, then steps back and becomes involved only for troubleshooting purposes.

There is, of course, no right answer, except the one that works in the particular organization. It *is* important, however, that the training department makes sure that it and everyone else involved clearly understands the role it intends to play.

Summary

To be really successful, a mentoring programme must obtain acceptance and commitment from participants and non-participants alike. The scheme should have empathetic, carefully selected and trained mentors, protégés who understand how to make the most of opportunities, and clear goals accepted by all. A great deal of effort is therefore needed to prepare employees at all levels for the introduction of the programme, ensuring that everyone knows what is happening, why and how the scheme will work. Particular attention should be given to the mentoring pairs, the protégé's boss and the protégé's peers. Starting small with a modest experiment helps take some of the bugs out of the system before it is applied generally throughout the organization.

Chapter 8
Running the mentoring programme

The relationship should develop swiftly and smoothly if both mentor and protégé have been well selected and well prepared. The phases the relationship typically goes through are examined in the next chapter. In this short section we look at how to make sure that the mentoring pair make the most of the opportunity given them.

By the time the mentor and protégé hold their first formal meeting under the mentoring programme, both should have a clear idea of the objectives of the relationship. These may be relatively vague at this stage, not least because the programme is intended to help the protégé refine and develop his career objectives. However, they should at least start with some form of assessment of the younger person's strengths and weaknesses, either provided by an assessment centre, or by routine performance appraisal with the protégé's boss. They will also, of course, take into account the general programme objectives, which both parties should understand clearly.

Typical starting objectives might be:

1 Introduce the protégé to other, parallel functions or departments whose work he will need to understand to progress, or which may open his eyes to potential sideways moves.
2 Identify and assign to the protégé a challenging project that will stretch him in areas where he needs to develop his ability. This project, often shared with the mentor, gives the protégé a clear aim which helps open the relationship up.
3 Increase the protégé's visibility in areas of the company where it will aid his career prospects.
4 Establish a self-study programme targeted to the protégé's individual needs.

70

A large UK chemical company sets out the following responsibilities at the beginning of a mentoring relationship:

- Meet the protégé once a month for an hour by timetabling formally in advance
- Ensure the protégé maintains a brief diary of daily events to form the basis for the monthly discussion
- Develop a personal relationship with the protégé
- Maintain the relationship for two years.

The objectives will be defined and adopted as the relationship develops and as the protégé needs change. It is also expected that the two people start off with the same understanding of the ground rules of the relationship. In particular there have to be clear rules of behaviour. One short but effective set of rules states:

1   The mentor will only enquire or intrude into the protégé's personal life by invitation.
2   The mentor will not make excessive demands on the protégé's time.
3   The protégé will not make excessive demands on the mentor's time.
4   The protégé will only use the mentor's authority with the mentor's consent.
5   The mentor will assist the protégé in achieving his objectives, but will let the protégé run his own show as much as possible.

Another common guideline is: 'The mentor will only communicate his knowledge of the protégé to other parties with the protégé's consent.'

Some organizations provide a general set of core rules for all mentoring relationships; others leave it to the individuals to decide. Whichever route they choose, the aim is to help the protégé stand on his own feet, not to make him dependent. As the relationship develops, the mentor must give the protégé frank advice and observations on his progress towards the objectives they have agreed.

A regular progress review, probably monthly at first, then gradually extending to as long as six-monthly, needs to be formalized. Company policy will decide whether the results of this review are confidential to the pair or communicated to the personnel department. All the roles of the mentor, as discussed in chapter 5, now come into play.

Monitoring the programme

The company also needs some system of feedback and evaluation in order to know whether the mentoring relationship is functioning efficiently and successfully. For example, one large UK manufacturing company holds a graduate workshop at least once a year, so that protégés can get together and produce a report recommending changes in the system.

If there is a careful monitoring system there will always be up-to-date information for the co-ordinators to decide whether to retain, expand, adjust or terminate the arrangement. To do this a company can:

1   Build check-points into the programme by arranging regular meetings with the mentors and co-ordinators, as well as mini-reports and memos, so that all the participants can express their opinions about the programme. The NHS in Wales has a Management Development Officer with overall responsibility for the programme, who visits the mentor every 3–4 months to assess the protégé's progress and ensure the relationship is working. Experience has shown this allows difficulties to be dealt with promptly.
2   Encourage protégés to write up reports describing mentoring activities and what they learnt from them.
3   Arrange evaluation meetings between protégés and mentors so that they can exchange perceptions and criticisms, give recognition to well executed jobs and identify areas where problems might arise.
4   Issue a company questionnaire to allow mentoring participants to evaluate the outcome of the programme.
5   Collect data that will show if the programme has made a significant contribution to participants' careers. Information on promotions, transfers, salary increases and career decisions allows the company to plot the career paths of mentors and protégés once they leave the programme.

These results may be compared to a random sample of employees who are at similar stages of their careers.

BP Chemicals is unusual in that it audits its scheme annually, both to improve the scheme and to demonstrate that the company takes mentoring seriously. The audit shows mentoring works best when:

- Graduates meet their mentors shortly after arriving on site
- Early meetings are regular and the mentors appear purposeful and confident
- The relationship feels 'real'
- The mentor and protégé are on the same site but in different parts of the company
- Both mentor and protégé start with the premise that mentoring is 'good'
- The mentor is not a line manager to the protégé
- Graduates use diary notes to discuss what they have been doing since the last meeting.

Some practical suggestions

1   Arrange for the mentor and protégé to be involved in some of the same projects. Working together temporarily helps the mentor and protégé to understand better the methods and style each employs at work. Projects also allow the protégés to produce visible results.
2   Take protégés to formal and informal management meetings. Always hold debriefing sessions afterwards.
3   Arrange visits for the protégés to various parts of the organization to broaden their perspectives of how the organization functions and what are the other organizational goals.
4   Keep each phase of the programme short. Six months is a suitable time, since it is long enough for a company to assess the impact it has made on the organization and recognize alterations which need to be implemented.

Summary

The mentoring programme needs considerable maintenance; it cannot be left to its own devices. Monitoring of progress versus regularly reviewed objectives is essential to ensure that protégé, mentor and company all benefit from the scheme.

Chapter 9
Phases of the mentoring relationship

The relationship with the mentor influences the career and personal development of a young employee. In the early stages of his career the young employee's identity, career aspirations and business relationships are forming. The junior must learn new technical, political and interpersonal skills. Throughout this process, the mentor relationship is often the most important vehicle for stimulating and assisting his development. The mentor:

offers friendship
acts as a role model
accepts and confirms the protégé's notions about his own identity
supports him
gives him confidence and a feeling of competence.

The mentor also finds that a relationship with a younger employee answers certain of his own psychological needs. The mid-career stage can be difficult for many executives as they find there is little chance of any further growth or advancement. The mentor's career may be in danger of stagnation as he feels he is locked into a pattern of repetition and uniformity. Entering a mentoring relationship at that stage of the mentor's career provides him with refreshing new challenges. He can redirect his energies into a stimulating and creative role.

Mentoring demands a flexible and individual approach rather than applying old, well-used formulae. As a result, the mentor finds new self respect as he recognizes he has valuable experiences and knowledge to pass on to the protégé.

A major study into the nature of the mentoring process was conducted in the early 1980s by Katherine Kram, Assistant

Professor of Organizational Behaviour at Boston University's School of Management. Kram attempted to discover the significance of the relationship for the mentor and the protégé and how mentoring influenced each party's career and self development. She also tried to establish whether mentoring relationships share any similar characteristics.

Kram conducted her survey in a public utility company of 15,000 employees, in the North East region of the United States. She studied 18 mentoring pairs, using in-depth interviews. The young protégés' ages ranged between 26 and 34, while the mentors' ages ranged between 39 and 63. The relationships varied considerably in duration, but Kram found that they were on average about five years long. Each relationship generally progressed through four distinct stages.

The start of the relationship

During the first six months to a year of a successful mentoring relationship, the young protégé may well hold an unrealistically ideal picture of his mentor. He frequently sees the mentor as an extremely competent figure, who gives him support and guidance. In these circumstances the protégé identifies strongly with his mentor and draws emotional support from the relationship. The young manager feels he is cared for by someone of great importance within the organization.

The opposite, of course, may also occasionally be the case. A protégé may begin the relationship with a great deal of suspicion and an image of the more senior manager as a 'played out time-server'. How well the mentoring relationship works here will depend on whether the mentor wins the protégé's respect as the nature of the job he does and the difficulty of the decisions he takes become clearer.

For the mentor, the relationship with his protégé can also be highly rewarding during this period. He is drawn to the protégé because of his potential and willingness to learn, seeing in him someone to whom he can pass on his own values and perspectives. In a successful relationship, mentors also derive satisfaction from recognizing how they can speed the protégé's growth by supplying advice and support. Many mentors also comment on the sense of pride they have in seeing their protégés progress. Both mentor and protégé develop positive expectations of each other. By the end of the first year they have gained sufficient confidence in each other and in the relationship to set into motion more substantial arrangements for opportunities for tutorage.

The middle period

The middle period lasts for two to five years and is the most rewarding for the two parties. The relationship is cultivated as the mentor coaches and promotes his protégé. The friendship between the two strengthens as a high degree of trust and intimacy builds up between the mentor and protégé.

The mentor's ability to coach the protégé and clarify his sense of purpose and identity helps to improve the young person's sense of self worth. The mentor provides him with work opportunities which help to develop his managerial skills and confirm and reinforce his sense of competence and ability. The protégé understands the business scenario better and knows how to control his work environment.

One protégé commented:

> I was very under-confident when I joined this company. I was newly divorced and I had not worked for quite some time. I was wholly intimidated by the business world. My mentor encouraged me to perform beyond my job description. She would criticize my performance, explain my mistakes and advise me on how to perform better. Above all she gave me confidence. She would say 'I know that you have the ability to do it, and I know that you *will* do it.' Her encouragement and faith in me was a great support and incentive.

It is at this stage that the mentor gains the most satisfaction from the knowledge that he has had an important effect on the protégé's development. One mentor tries to describe the pride he feels when he sees his protégé perform well and receive recognition from the company, in this way: 'The satisfaction I receive is similar to parental pride. You have put faith in that person and helped him develop. When

he succeeds you feel it has all been worthwhile and you
remember that you were instrumental in helping him to do
so.'

Mentors also receive technical and psychological help and
support from their protégés. The protégé now has the skill to
help his mentor as well as the ability to recognize the needs of
the senior executive. The mentor has a renewed sense of his
own influence and power as he opens doors in the organization
for his protégé. He also feels he is passing something to the
company which will have lasting value. Through the protégé,
the mentor can express his own perspectives and values.

At this stage the relationship is particularly rich for both
the mentor and protégé. The mutual confidence that develops
between the two people gives the protégé the confidence to
challenge the mentor's ideas, just as his own are challenged
by the mentor. This high level of intellectual involvement
can be very productive in terms of new ways of looking at
old problems.

By now, the mentor and the protégé will have agreed upon
a career path, involving at least one and usually several clearly
defined promotional or horizontal moves. The first of these
moves may even have been taken.

Discussions between the mentor and protégé now centre
less on defining objectives than on strategies and tactics to
achieve them. Project work which the mentor sets his protégé
is aimed both at developing skills and at assessing how well
they have been absorbed. The two people meet regularly
to review progress in each area where they have agreed
improvement is necessary to qualify for the next career step.
The mentor directs the protégé towards additional sources of
learning and challenges him to prove the successes he claims.

Dissolving the relationship

After two to five years the mentoring relationship begins
to draw apart. The mentor and the protégé are affected by
organizational changes. The protégé has advanced sufficiently
to be experiencing new independence and autonomy. The
mentor relationship becomes less essential to him as he needs
change.

Protégés may respond differently when the relationship

declines according to how prepared they are for the separation. If a change in career position occurs before the protégé feels ready to operate independently of his mentor, he will experience a time of uncertainty and anxiety. He will miss the psychological support of the mentor and be aware that he no longer has a 'safety net' to fall upon if he makes a wrong decision. The unprepared protégé can also feel abandoned and betrayed and lose confidence.

One young British protégé found her first year apart from her mentor a very difficult time emotionally. A period of redefinition was necessary as she had to demonstrate to the rest of the organization that she was able to operate independently without her mentor. 'I had to prove to myself and the rest of the company that it was my ability which got me my new job and not my mentor's influence. I had to show I could stand alone. I think the whole process helped me to mature. Now if I have any difficulties I rely on myself.'

If the protégé is fully prepared for separation from his mentor, he enjoys his new found freedom and independence. It is a little like driving the car home after having passed the driving test.

Most mentors accept that their protégés must move away from them in the company and become psychologically more self sufficient. Even after the separation has taken place, the mentor continues to encourage his protégé to move forward in his career. He will often promote the protégé at a distance and be kept informed of his progress.

However, some mentors are unwilling to allow their protégés to go beyond their influence and control. This is most common in senior executives who are insecure in their own positions. The mentor tends to project his own negative career expectations onto the protégé. If he feels he can go no higher in the company he is unlikely to feel that a subordinate will either.

Some managers whose own careers have stagnated and offer little hope for future advancement resent a protégé who has more career opportunities. This kind of mentor does not want the protégé to outstrip him and as a result attempts to delay the protégé's movement, by insisting the protégé stay in the same position.

Where the protégé feels ready to break the mentoring relationship but is unable to move beyond the mentor's sphere of influence, he may feel frustrated, restless and ultimately hostile. This is another argument against the use of the immediate boss as a mentor. While such feelings can be absorbed across departmental boundaries, they may be explosive within the department. Some companies use the personnel department, the project controller or an arbitrator in senior management to ensure that the protégé has someone to appeal to if conflict of this kind arises. (The mentor, too can use this formal route to express his disquiet if he believes a protégé is being pushed too fast for his own good.) Such arbitration is rare, however, not least because the numbers of people involved in most companies are sufficiently small for the issues to be resolved by informal means.

For both the mentor and the protégé the period of divorce and separation is important for their reputation and career in the organization. The protégé demonstrates his skills and independence while the mentor shows to colleagues and other potential protégés that he develops young people successfully. The progress of the protégé proves the accuracy of the mentor's insight into potential.

By now, the protégé's career objectives may have changed several times, as the mentor has made him aware of new opportunities and expected changes in the organization. The protégé will have gradually assumed more and more of the responsibility for his own career objectives and will increasingly be taking the initiative in seeking out training opportunities and experience that will help him achieve his goals. In effect, the mentor has taught him what he knows and there is little more to pass on.

Restarting the relationship

Both protégé and mentor continue to have some form of interaction, although it is on a more casual basis and is usually restricted to specific projects. At AMI Healthcare, for example, the mentoring relationships often continue after the programme has ended as mentors continue to help protégés with the personal development plans they drew up. The relationship enters a new stage where the protégé and mentor regard each other as equals. The relationship now develops into a friendship with the two maintaining contact with each other on the basis of mutual advantage rather than upon the primarily one-sided career advantage once offered.

The protégé now ceases to identify with the mentor, whose weaknesses he now recognizes alongside the strengths that had seemed so impressive in the early stages of the relationship. The bond of gratitude takes over from the bond of need. When the two become peers in the organization, uncertainty and discomfort may occur as they adjust to the new role relationship.

This new transition can also be characterized by hostility and resentment between the protégé and the mentor. The protégé may have found it difficult to make a complete break from the mentor. When the two meet again on a more equal footing, the protégé often feels that he will fall into the former dependent role. To prevent this, the protégé behaves aggressively to the mentor and the former intimacy is not re-established.

Summary

Clearly, every mentoring relationship is unique, just as every individual is unique. But a high proportion of relationships does seem to follow these basic stages of development. To minimize the problems and maximize the benefits of mentoring, both the mentor and the protégé need to be well briefed on how the relationship may develop. The company, too, needs to monitor the stages of development to provide the external support that will head off serious problems before they occur.

Chapter 10
Problems of the mentoring relationship

While mentoring is a powerful human resource development tool, it is only one of many in the corporate tool-box. Badly handled, it can turn into a spanner in the works. Even well handled, it is not appropriate in all circumstances, nor is it necessarily superior to other forms of management development. Rather, it is a process to be used alongside other, more traditional forms of career progression. Many American companies, which have been running mentoring programmes during the last decade, now encourage managers to have as many developmental relationships of different kinds as possible.

Katherine Kram puts the negative side of a whole-hearted corporate commitment to mentoring. 'The concept has become too aggrandized. Mentoring can sometimes be limited in value or even destructive in a company. Career development staff should remember that other relationships, for example with peers, can be just as rewarding and fruitful as mentoring relationships.'

Some companies have found the main problem is the unfamiliarity of mentoring in the business environment. Other critics say true mentor/protégé relationships are rare and should not develop at gunpoint. Michael Zey, in his book *The Mentor Connection*, feels that trying to formalize 'what is at best a random occurence' can prove disastrous if management does not stand by the newly joined couples.

Some formal mentoring is seen as a quick fix for companies who should really be looking at changing their whole culture. Reba Keele, Assistant Professor of Organizational Behavior at Brigham Young University, Utah, feels that formal mentoring, like arranged marriages, works better in Far Eastern cultures than Western. In Japan especially, she points out, the traditional respect for age and experience provides a framework that most people can accept. As far as the mentors are concerned:

> In the Japanese organization, the senior member of management has already accepted the fact that he is not going to become the next president. Assuming the responsibility of mentoring is considered an honor and recognition of your status. Whereas in our organizations, issues that have to do with human resource development are not considered primary functions.

Organizations should monitor the programme carefully so that they can identify and solve problems swiftly. Most difficulties can easily be resolved if they are recognized early and brought out into the open. Clear lines of communication between mentors, protégés and programme co-ordinators can ensure that dissatisfactions with the relationship will result in immediate action.

Some of the most frequent problems include:

1 Power alignments

By assigning a mentor to a protégé in a different department or a different division, a company changes the nature of its informal structure. Close relationships which extend beyond the normal business restraints and which cut across the barrier of status and position mean that new alliances are formed between junior and senior employees. A company which has run a mentoring programme for several years may have the additional power nexus of a former mentor and a protégé, now on the same organizational rung, actively promoting and assisting each other. While this means the informal communications of a company are strengthened, it can also lead to an increase in corporate politics.

One of the objectives of the mentoring programme is at least partly to overcome the unfairness of the informal old boy networks. Unless the company is vigilant, there is a very real danger that, instead of making the system more open and fair, the scheme may simply create new closed networks. If covert sources of information are available only to the chosen few, within mentor/protégé relationships, only the initiated know how to gain and use company resources effectively. Through this, mentors and protégés can form a small yet powerful group capable of operating through and beyond the company's formal positions of power.

Before BP Chemicals began its mentoring programme, doubters thought it would interfere with the authority and skills of the line manager and would set up a network independent of management control. In practice, these fears proved groundless, to the extent that the pilot plant's managers changed from sceptics to enthusiasts.

Failure to make it clear from the outset that the young manager is still primarily responsible to his immediate boss and not to his mentor can create serious power-play problems. The mentor has to guard against creating situations where the protégé uses his special relationship to bypass the authority of his boss. At the same time, the mentor himself must not override the protégé's boss, other than in exceptional cases. Unfortunately, obscuring the company's command structure can happen all too easily. Because the mentor and protégé are adhering to a different system of loyalty and authority, they cut across the recognized formal hierarchy. An invisible chain of command can emerge subtly to challenge the established one, resulting in confusion, conflict and bitterness.

The protégé's immediate superior can often be placed in an uncomfortable and difficult position by all this. A brittle relationship can develop between the protégé, his manager and the mentor if the manager is excluded from the relationship. The manager in this situation feels threatened and frequently resents the mentor's behaviour, interpreting it as open interference. If the mentor overrides the manager's authority, the latter will feel his authority is being publicly undermined. Inevitably, he will resort to obstructing the mentoring relationship in order to protect his own position. An experienced mentoring scheme administrator, quoted in a US newsletter, points out that it's only natural for the protégé's boss, who after all has a department to run, to be jealous of the mentor's influence – especially if the mentor has a powerful position in the organization. 'Remember that the boss is the boss,' he advises would-be mentors. 'And don't let your own experiences blind you to the realities. The last thing a protégé needs is advice from the mentor that leads to conflict with the supervisor.'

In one company, a protégé's manager reacted strongly against a mentor who was grooming a 'fast track' employee. The mentor would often decide that the protégé should accompany him on company conferences, without consulting the protégé's supervisor. In the end the manager felt so overshadowed by the mentor that he insisted the protégé needed to attend to immediate work and did not have the available time for conferences. This open conflict need not have occurred if the mentor had exercised more sensitivity and diplomacy. The line manager should be involved from the very beginning. One company asks line managers to take prospective protégés to the mentor's office for the first meeting. And in Midland Bank's IT department line managers and mentors are briefed together by a senior executive.

In companies where there are a large number of middle manager positions and few senior positions, mentors again need to conduct their mentoring relationships carefully. A manager who is unlikely to be promoted further may resent the protégé beneath him being groomed for advancement. The manager will realize he has been passed over by the company and could possibly attempt to hinder the protégé's prospects by writing unfavourable reports. In this situation the mentor and the protégé need to try to make the relationship between them as invisible as possible.

2 Work organization problems

The protégé may sometimes channel his energies into activities that he thinks will please his mentor, at the expense of the daily routines of the job that he is paid to do. Once again, this can cause severe resentment and opposition from the protégé's immediate boss. In addition, both the mentor's colleagues and the protégé's peers may feel the selection was unjustified if there is no visible evidence of excellence in the protégé's normal work.

3 Problems with the selection process

Kram points out that, unless the formal mentoring programme is handled very publicly, with transparent and fair selection procedures, it may demotivate those excluded from the club. Since most organizations have a pyramidal structure, it follows that there will always be some junior managers who have a mentor and some who do not. 'There are just not enough mentors to go around,' she explains, 'so a company faces the constant danger of alienating failed candidates.'

Unfortunately the resentment and disappointment felt by failed applicants can outweigh the benefits which successful candidates receive from the programme. A junior who does not gain entry all too often believes the selectors' decision to be based on his own personal limitations, rather than due to a lack of programme resources. He believes that it is an unspoken statement by the company indicating that he lacks the ability to fill important positions in the future. In short he has been given a vote of 'no confidence'.

One UK company with a number of geographically spread operations invited applications for the pilot of its mentoring programme. More than forty people applied for the fifteen available places. Although the company wrote to all the unsuccessful candidates, suggesting they speak to their local employee counsellor, only one did so – and she handed in her notice. The company learned that it had to:

- make sure everyone knew the criteria for selection
- demonstrate that mentoring was just one route to advancement among many
- consider unsuccessful candidates' reactions at a much earlier stage.

Such negative experiences can be very damaging to a junior manager. His self-confidence and morale may be eroded to the extent that he underrates his own ability and potential. He lowers his career aspirations accordingly. As a result, instead of having a motivated young employee who aims at promotion through a high standard of work, a company has an individual whose enthusiasm is curbed and who ceases to stretch his abilities because there seems to be no reward in doing so.

Alternatively, a failed candidate can feel resentment and bitterness as he sees his peers receive treatment which seems 'preferential'. 'Favouritism' is a frequently heard complaint, as well as the accusation that peers used unfair tactics to gain a place on the programme. A protégé's friendship with a senior executive becomes 'sucking up' or 'crawling'. Envy and resentment from a protégé's peers can frequently hinder or even destroy a mentoring programme.

It is probably not possible to assure everyone that the selection process has been totally fair and there will always be a few individuals who convince themselves that the programme caters only for those who are best at impressing the right people rather than those who are most able and deserving.

It is for this reason that General Motors Corp disdains mentoring programmes altogether. The company believes that mentoring is not based on a strict system of meritocracy. 'Instead of grooming crown princes we scrutinize each employee through an elaborate system of annual review', explains William Mackinnon, general director for worldwide personnel administration. The company aims to foster an egalitarian attitude in its organization and believes that mentoring can hinder that objective.

Company morale suffers considerably if it is generally believed that promotions are no longer linked to performance. Entire generations of employees can come to feel that what counts is not the ability to do the job, but how well you can play corporate politics.

All this suggests that companies must provide scrupulously fair and public methods of selection for mentoring programmes or, for that matter, for any other management development process that creates an élite corps. Crude methods of selection are a recipe for disaster within a mentoring programme. Katherine Kram points out that many mentors choose protégés on the basis of remarkably superficial impressions. 'When I asked executives why they were interested in certain young managers, I was frequently told, because I had heard he had a lot of potential. Once they have been adopted as protégés, the expectation becomes self-fulfilling.'

Because these young managers succeed in climbing the corporate ladder, programme selectors may easily be misled into thinking the scheme is working well, whereas in fact there may be a significant waste of talent. But the protégé's peers are sure to recognize and resent the limitations and unfairness of the programme.

Another danger of a mentoring programme is that it

may help to perpetuate stereotypes both in a company's management style and in its culture. Ideas and values which senior executives pass down to protégés may in reality be obsolete or irrelevant. If these values are too vigorously imposed, junior employees are discouraged from finding their own methods and instead use old solutions for new problems. As a result, the company becomes entrenched in the past and loses its ability to react quickly to the demands of the present.

4 Problems between mentor and protégé

Mentoring relationships do not always succeed. One common cause of failure, for example, is a simple mismatch between the protégé and mentor. They may not be able to feel at ease with one another, or to achieve the level of friendship necessary for rich communication. Thomas Taggart, an administrative official at the Bank of America, points out that stunted communications between protégé and mentor contributed to the failure of the bank's mentoring programme. At monthly luncheons with their protégés, busy executives were often unable to break through the formality of the meeting. Taggart comments 'After the polite "How are you?" and the perfunctory "fine thanks" response, there was little to say. The parties simply did not have similar jobs or work experiences to share.'

Executives who have heavy work loads and a full timetable may be just too pressurized to develop their mentoring relationships fully. Bennett Dolin, vice-president for personnel development at Security Pacific Bank comments on the failure of some mentors to establish a real rapport with their protégé: 'Some mentors were simply too harrassed by work to do a proper job. So in some cases we arranged for the mentor to be changed.'

One protégé had an unrewarding relationship with a senior executive. He recalls:

> I did not have a very close relationship with my mentor. Eventually, half way through the programme I was forced to change mentors. He was assigned to a new job and was inundated with work. I had no chance to get

to know him and anyway he did not think that I needed a mentor. The relationship appeared to add little value to my career.

Mentor relationships can fail when the protégé expects or demands too much from his mentor. When he realizes the mentor is unable to transform his career, the protégé may feel resentful and betrayed. Katherine Kram explains:

> Having a mentor is not the only way of moving up within a company. Establishing good relationships with other managers as well as peers constructs a constellation of relationships which is just as valuable, or even more useful. Any one relationship will inevitably contain flaws.

Protégés need to be realistic from the beginning, she says. They should not expect the relationship to meet every need, nor for it to continue indefinitely. 'Mentors provide different degrees of mentoring and the protégé should accept this,' she maintains.

Another problem is that the mentor may cling to his protégé and be unwilling to let him become independent. A divisional manager wished to move to headquarters and could not understand why the company was so reluctant to transfer him.

> I begged the powers that be to move me, yet they refused to alter their position. I was mystified until a colleague told me that my mentor had insisted that I was not ready for the move. The only thing I could do was to make it clear to him that I was grateful for all the help he had given my career, yet nevertheless I was determined to move on – or move out. He denied any involvement, but a month later I was transferred. The evidence seemed to speak for itself.

Mentors, being human, inevitably make mistakes. Some mentors cross a fine line too easily between exhibiting confidence in a protégé and expecting too much. One young executive was forced to leave his job because of the unbearable pressure his mentor unknowingly placed upon him. He explains:

> He seemed to think I could do anything that he asked me
> to do. Eventually it got to the stage where I was terrified
> he would discover I was not a whiz kid and was in fact
> quite average. My position was made so unbearable by
> my mentor that I decided to quit.

Had his mentor directed him towards additional training
in key areas he might well have gained the confidence to
cope.

At the other extreme, some mentors can dominate their
protégés, leaving them little space for their own thoughts.
In practice, most protégés are sufficiently mature and determined to ignore this kind of pressure, but it can nonetheless
be a problem for people who are not strong-willed or who
start with a low level of self-confidence.

Some mentors may have insufficient understanding of
the company. Larry Greiner, Professor of Organizational
Behaviour at the University of Southern California, recalls an
incident:

> A senior manager counselled his protégé to stay in
> marketing, when in reality the real avenue for advance-
> ment in the firm was through manufacturing. The protégé
> relied solely on his mentor's advice and did as he was told.
> The result was a stagnant career.

A mentor may also damage the protégé's career if he does
not consider properly or understand the younger person's
skills and interests. He may urge the junior into assignments
which do not suit his abilities. The protégé then finds himself
trapped in work situations which do not demonstrate his
full ability, making his next career steps difficult if not
impossible.

Protégés who are involved in a highly visible mentor
relationship can also damage their mentor's career and
reputation. The mentor may be discredited in the organization
if his protégé fails dramatically in an important project. Mud
sticks at the top of the tree, too.

In some cases, mistakes by the protégé may cause the
mentor to withdraw from the role to save his own reputation,
leaving the protégé to sink or swim on his own. Alternatively

the fear of damage to his reputation can cause a mentor to attempt to camouflage his protégé's mistakes and protect him from the consequences of his errors. Rather than coach the protégé or allow him to be demoted to a position more suited to his competence, the mentor indirectly assists the decline of staff quality in the organization.

Similarly, the protégé's career will be adversely affected if his mentor loses organizational credibility. Lynn Gilbert, head of executive recruiters, Gilbert Tweed Associates, explains:

> There is a real risk in being identified as somebody's protégé. Many individuals suffer rather than benefit by having a mentor. If the latter falls out of favour in a company there is a strong likelihood that the protégé will also do so.

Surprisingly, there is relatively little evidence of breaches of confidentiality between mentor and protégé. One large company, which has surveyed all its mentors and protégés, found only one instance of an indiscreet mentor, and none of the protégés betraying their mentors' confidences. Some companies go to considerable lengths to avoid the possibility of inadvertent passing on of confidential information. In Midland Bank's IT department, for example, says Employee Development Manager Mike Killingley:

> Any feedback from the mentoring relationship which the mentor wishes to get back to the line manager will not be given direct (to avoid the 'big brother' factor) but by a member of the mentor's peer group who is the line manager's boss and a mentor himself.

The NHS in Wales has encountered the following difficulties with mentoring:

- time availability – demand can be underestimated
- lethargy – the relationship can become complacent
- flexibility – this can be required if the mentor and protégé do not match up to each others' expectations
- over-caution – not allowing the relationship to grow
- personality clashes – in the last resort a new mentor

will be found and counselling given by the Management Development Officer to the trainee
- lack of confidentiality
- balancing professionalism and friendship.

What the surveys say

The 1987 PA survey identifies four significant general problems, which occur in mentoring programmes across the world. In order of frequency, these are:

- inadequate definition of mentor-protégé roles
- level of commitment
- lack of continuity for training programme to post-training career
- resentment from protégé's line manager.

The study also found that company culture could be a major hurdle: 'If little trust exists between levels of management and people are used to direction, with little scope for initiative, mentoring relationships will be difficult to establish.'

It also identified eight failed schemes, most of which simply ran out of steam after three to four years. Of these failures, "50% . . . were considered to be largely successful when they were running", and more than half of the companies thought they would probably consider reintroducing a scheme in the future.'

The 1989 Industrial Society/ITEM survey found that problems with mentoring programmes included:

> inability to give negative feedback constructively; time constraints on mentors; mismatches between mentors and protégés; and frequent moves of site that mean mentor and protégé have to be changed.

However, most companies had experienced very few problems.

Summary

Mentoring should not be the only form of career development

within the organization. The company must also be aware of the problems and the conflicts that the mentoring pair may experience with the protégé's boss and peers. Careful selection and preparation of both mentor and protégé can avoid both these problems and others that may arise with the mentoring relationship itself.

Chapter 11
The special issue of male/female mentoring

The increasing numbers of women now entering careers in management suffer from a major disadvantage: by and large they are not exposed to the same range of experiences and career opportunities as men. While formal barriers have been reduced through legislation, women continue to be hindered in their careers by invisible obstacles such as prejudice and distrust. As the demand for quality white collar management increases, the need for organizations to question why there are so few women in management will become acute.

If women managers are accepted in the formal structure of the organization, in the informal social structure they can still be looked on with suspicion. The masculine culture of a company may mean that women are not fully integrated; in a sense they are still regarded as outsiders or interlopers.

Low expectations or stereotyped images can often mean that women managers are delegated undemanding jobs, making them less visible than male managers. Women may be expected to perform tasks which are seen as suitably 'feminine' in nature, such as personnel, rather than the more 'masculine' managerial jobs such as financial analysis. As a result, women managers frequently lack opportunities to develop a wide range of managerial skills.

Dr Judi Marshall of Bath University found that mentoring improved the promotion prospects of women managers. Interviewing thirty women managers from middle management to director level Marshall found that 70% either were currently or had been in a mentoring relationship. All of these women placed great value on the relationship and said it had been a very important factor in their career development, she explained. The majority of the surveyed women saw visibility as a crucial factor for success. The mentors sponsored the women and often nominated them for

94

promotion committees when they would not have normally been considered for posts. If a mentor vouches for a woman manager companies are more willing to promote her because they view the mentor as a 'safety net', she concludes.

Agnes Missiran found that most successful women in corporate America credited their mentors with helping them to succeed. 'I think sponsored women especially need a mentor, because the mentor demonstrates what they can become. I would like to see more women mentors,' declares Clair Macintyre, a past ICI protégé and now a mentor herself.

Jenny Blake, an independent consultant, comments:

> I think the mentoring relationship is very beneficial to both the protégé and the mentor. In my capacity as a consultant I now try to fill the mentor role. I mentor personnel trainers and help them with their own development. At the moment I am mentoring a senior manager in the probationary service. I feel an older woman can play a very positive role as a mentor. I do not appear threatening to men, so I receive open feedback. I have found that an increasing number of women in their late 30s and 40s are now willing to be mentors. They want to act as a role model to younger women to demonstrate that women can succeed in business. It seems clear to me that mentoring can and will play a very positive role in the future.

Says a woman manager working for a multinational company:

> While I worked for this company, I had two mentors, both male and both 15–20 years older than I. The first mentor was invaluable in my early career because he taught me so much about the 'right' way to get on politically. He saw that my abilities were acknowledged, that I was promoted and given credit for my accomplishments and that I was delegated considerable responsibilities.
>
> My first mentor also served as a role model. What I learned from working for him made me a good manager and considerably helped to advance my career. He encouraged me to compete in the corporation and strive to go up the career ladder. I still heed his advice of long ago in numerous situations.
>
> After five years in the domestic operation, I went into the international section, where I met my second mentor.

He was a senior executive and 20 years my senior. He taught me everything he knew about conducting oneself in business, which is sometimes worth more than any actual skill. He was important for my career because he defended my interests in a very male chauvinist environment.

I also tried to have the chief executive as my mentor. Believe me, I tried cultivating the relationship – not in a flirtatious way but by presenting myself as a serious, loyal and hard-working manager. He had his own protégés, however, all male.

My two successful mentor relationships were very similar. I would be lying if I did not admit that I was very instrumental in developing and maintaining the relationships for my own advantage. Because I was in the corporate rat race, I naturally gravitated towards those in power who would help me rise, but I liked and respected both of these men. The relationships were businesslike and professional, but there's no doubt that I used whatever advantage I had as a younger, attractive and intelligent woman.*

Male-female mentoring

Male-female mentoring assists women managers primarily because it influences the informal as well as the formal structure of an organization. A structured career programme only yields marginal benefits to women managers because it cannot easily influence the invisible social life of a company. A mentoring programme works at a more informal level because a close relationship must be forged between a mentor and a protégé. This gradually breaks down any preconceptions or sexual prejudices either may have. For a woman protégé the mentor relationship:

1 Gives her a legitimate access to key male executives who have the power to facilitate her career. If a woman approached a male executive outside a mentoring programme it could

---

* Reproduced from David Clutterbuck and Marion Devine (eds), *Businesswoman* (Macmillan, 1987)

be interpreted as sexually provocative behaviour in an organization with strong sexual stereotypes.

2   Increases her visibility in an organization. Her mentor supplies her with opportunities to prove herself. A young female protégé working in social services comments: 'My male mentor has helped me to be taken seriously in the organization. There are a large number of women in the middle section, but only one woman at the top.'

One woman protégé discovered by Zey worked in an account group at an advertising agency. As the only woman in the team, she was excluded from key informal meetings with company supervisors and could not gain access to networks that operated by invitation only. She was also excluded from important informal client meetings in case they went on for drinks and she did not fit in. 'In an advertising account group your success depends on getting yourself noticed by senior management. I had male peers who were often invited out by the boss for a drink, or a game of golf. I was never asked.' When she moved to her next company she had learned enough about corporate politics to know she needed a mentor.

3   Bestows legitimacy upon her. The mentor's attention to her career is a public gesture of support and informs the rest of the company that senior management believes she is worth the investment of time and energy. One female protégé commented: 'Managers tend to flirt with female staff and rarely think of them as potential managers or directors. It is usually male employees who obtain the more important and influential positions. These ingrained ideas make it harder for women to succeed. My mentor is teaching me to show upper management that I am serious about my career. It seems to be working so far.'

Pauline works in the London headquarters of a nationalized industry. While the industry has changed from a predominantly heavy labour, dirty occupation to a relatively clean and less labour-intensive operation, the strong male orientation and a high degree of chauvinism have continued almost unabated.

Pauline was the first woman to reach senior officer grade. 'I faced considerable hostility in the company; some I knew of and some my mentor shielded me from. There was widespread doubt about a woman's competence for the job. I doubt that I would have been promoted if I had not had a mentor behind me.'

The strongest opposition came from directors' secretaries who felt themselves top of the pecking order. Pauline's mentor learnt he had to enlist their support and often mentioned to them how wonderful it was to see a woman doing so well in the company. Eventually they gave Pauline their full support and through them directors heard how she was progressing.

'Thanks to my mentor's tactics I had no problem with visibility in the company, as some women do. He taught me how to sell myself and showed me how I could gain acceptance in the company. If I had not been mentored by him there would have been no-one to tell me what I was capable of achieving.'

4   Provides occasions for less inhibited interaction with a male superior.

Mentoring activities may take the form of meetings and discussion groups which are sexually neutral. If there is not a formal mentoring programme an executive might attempt to get to know a promising junior socially through male-orientated activities, such as golf, squash, or having a drink together. If he attempted to use the same methods with a woman his intentions could easily be misinterpreted.

Paradoxically, Jenny Blake believes it can be easier for a woman to be adopted by a mentor than a man. 'I know that the two mentors I had in my past career actively sought the relationship because they felt it would not be competitive or threatening. They felt less secure about their relationships with other men because of the constant pressure to compete, so this made them reluctant to act as a mentor for younger men. What's more, the majority of companies have male-dominated upper levels, so a mentoring relationship with a woman can be refreshing and stimulating for the senior manager.' Just how widespread such attitudes are among male mentors is not known.

Potential problems with male/female mentoring

(a) Between the protégé and the mentor

A female protégé often experiences disappointment with the relationship because her male mentor is unable to meet all her developmental needs. She cannot emulate him fully and in certain areas may need to find her own methods of achieving goals and resolving problems. Marilyn Loden, author of *How to succeed in business without being one of the boys*, sees one example of this in the way women manage conflict. They put more emphasis than men on delegating or on group discussion. If the male mentor does not understand this, he may interpret it as lack of assertiveness and push the female protégé into signing up for an assertiveness course.

Sexual tensions between the two can inhibit the relationship and make it less rewarding than mentoring between two of the same sex.

Pressure to adopt established sexual roles sometimes causes tension and conflict in the relationship. A male mentor may feel overly protective towards a female mentor, and encourage her to be dependent. She may find it particularly difficult to terminate the relationship at the end of the mentoring pro-gramme. The same may also be true in the case of a female mentor and male protégé, especially where the age differences are similar to those in a mother/son relationship.

Says Dr Marilyn Puder-York, a clinical psychologist in New York:

> There are many very productive male-female mentoring relationships, but there must be a high sense of shared values and ethical behaviour on both sides.
>
> And you often have to counter society's perception of the relationship by having lunch instead of dinner and by including spouses in socializing. Otherwise both can pay a heavy price. In general, if a woman has a male mentor, she should seek out a woman mentor as well. Beyond the social considerations, there are politics for women that a man may not be aware of.

(b) Between the spouses and the mentoring pair

A mentoring relationship can seem threatening to the mentor's and protégé's partners, especially if business trips together are involved. The spouse often feels excluded by the closeness of the relationship.

Protégés have found various solutions, mostly based on total openness. Social gatherings where spouses are invited make a useful opportunity to demonstrate the businesslike nature of the relationship.

(c) Between the company and the mentoring pair

Sexual gossip and innuendo can kill a mentoring relationship before it gets going. Many potential male/female mentoring relationships never happen because of the fear of office gossip. In a mentoring programme it is often necessary for the two to work beyond work hours or even travel together. The two must act 'professionally' which can simply mean that behaviour has to be much more circumscribed than in a mentor relationship between two of the same sex. One mentor solved the problem of gossip. 'If you mentor one woman you are branded as a womanizer. If you mentor several, you are praised for your commitment to seeing more women in management.'

The extra visibility of the relationship in the company may discourage even the highest risk taker from being a mentor. 'A young man can have the luxury of failing quietly but a woman's mistakes are often broadcasted,' explains one mentor.

Both success and failure of the female protégé can harm the mentor's reputation. If she gains promotion, other employees may assume – in spite of all attempts to educate both sexes in the working environment in recent decades – she has procured it through sexual favours to senior management. If she fails, it is seen as a confirmation to senior management that the mentor was incorrect in his judgement and was initially influenced by sexual motives. Both outcomes are damaging to the mentor's career.

In the less common case where the mentor is a woman and the protégé a man, the culture of the organization may still inhibit the relationship. *Training and Development Journal*, in its May 1983 edition, quoted Carol Hunter of the Future's Group Inc, in these terms: ·

> She has observed cross-gender mentoring situations and has herself mentored men. She believes all cross-gender mentoring involves a good deal of risk.
>
> In many organizations it is not OK to share power and information with a woman and, thus, man-to-woman mentoring is highly suspect. Ironically, the sexual potential in the relationship is OK; it's a man-to-woman relationship other men understand. The man who doesn't take advantage of that option has lost his macho credentials and is doubly suspect.

The solutions

At all levels of the company and between the protégé and the mentor there must be:

communication
publicity
clarity
involvement.

A company must ensure that all of its employees are familiar with the process of mentoring. Information about the programme's objectives, methods and results help to minimize innuendo and suspicion in the company. Training sessions can help prepare the mentor and the protégé for the problems they may encounter and encourage each to have a realistic sense of the effectiveness of the programme. Mentors and protégés should arrange a meeting with their respective spouses at the start of the programme. As it proceeds they should communicate as much as possible to their partners about how the mentoring relationship is working.

What the surveys say

Relatively little was known about mentoring of women, and how (or if) it differed from men until 1987. In that year in the United States, the Center for Creative Leadership carried out interviews with male and female protégés. The centre concluded that a senior woman's career is likely to have been more deeply affected by mentoring than a senior man's. It also found that many women had their careers derailed before they reached executive level because they made political blunders, which they could have avoided with advice and guidance from a more senior manager.

In the UK, we carried out a survey of business women, with questionnaires sent to one hundred who had reached executive level inside a company and to one hundred women entrepreneurs. The response rate was a remarkable 49%. Among the key conclusions:

- Successful women managers are more likely than women entrepreneurs to have had a mentor (56% compared with 43%). One reason – possibly the most important – is that the entrepreneurs quit to set up on their own precisely because their progress was blunted in large corporations, through lack of a champion at higher levels
- 49% of the women had had a single mentor; 22% had had two; 21% had had three; and 8% had had four or five – or more – at different periods in their careers
- 94% of the women said their relationships were beneficial to their career
- More than half of the entrepreneurs' mentors had encouraged them to start their own businesses; 5% even helped them financially
- The vast majority of mentoring relationships (63%) started accidentally; only 8% of the women had actually approached their mentor
- The main benefits reported by the women were:
    — improved self-confidence and self-image
    — increased visibility to senior management (especially important to women managers)
    — focusing career aspirations
    — acting as a role model
    — help with work problems
    — improved communications and skills
- Most mentors (79%) were male
- More than two-fifths experienced no problems with the relationship; 37% had experienced problems of resentment

from peers; 5% said their careers had been damaged when their mentor lost credibility in the company
- two-thirds had experienced some form of sexual innuendo or gossip; 19% reported that their mentor's wife felt threatened by the relationship; 11% said their own husbands resented it; 4% said their mentor became too emotionally involved with them
- 60% of the women were acting as mentors themselves.

Summary

Male/female mentoring holds great promise as a means to create equal opportunity for women, but it poses special problems of gossip and personal behaviour. The solution is a high level of openness and communication with interested observers that leaves no room for rumour.

Chapter 12
Conclusion

In this relatively brief account of mentoring and how to implement a mentoring programme, we have inevitably raised a number of issues that warrant further discussion. Below we take up some of these in more detail.

1 All good mentoring relationships come to an end

While one person may have several mentors, each mentoring relationship must, as we saw in chapter 9, reach the stage where it is neither needed nor wanted any longer.

For this reason it is essential that each relationship is seen from the start as a temporary alignment. Elements of it may persist, in the form of mutual aid and friendship, for many years after, but there must be clear starting and finishing points. Probably the best pointer to the finishing point is when the protégé has achieved the medium-term objectives established early on in the relationship. A spokesman for Jewel Companies comments:

> We feel that after a couple of years the role loses its importance and may become a more negative element than a positive one. That is, after a few years in the business it is more important that an individual be achieving on his own rather than with the special help from a senior management level mentor.

However it is done, the two parties must be able to back out of the arrangement without recrimination where one or both feels it is no longer beneficial.

2 Good protégés often make good mentors

Many of the most successful mentors are people who have experienced mentoring from the other side. Indeed, it is possible for a manager to be simultaneously mentored from above while he mentors someone yet more junior.

One of the major difficulties in getting a mentoring programme off the ground is finding an adequate supply of mentors. Once the scheme has been going for many years, however, it automatically generates potential mentors from the ranks of former protégés. AMI Healthcare believes the acid test for the success of its mentoring programme is a continual supply of would-be mentors and protégés. Enthusiasm so far means the mentoring process has been self-perpetuating. If the mentoring philosophy can be infused into the corporate culture sufficiently, then it holds out the possibility that everyone can be mentored at some stage in their career.

3 Old stagers can benefit from mentors too

Mentoring should not be seen solely for young, relatively new recruits. There are frequently people in the organization whose development has been held back by circumstances other than ability. They may, for example, have had domestic ties which prevented them from demonstrating career ambition, particularly if they are married women. Or they may be in a cultural backwater in the company, out of the mainstream and in a staff position that has little interaction with key corporate functions.

4 How to find a mentor when the organization doesn't have a formal mentoring programme

Many people progress in their companies by seeking their own mentors. By and large, senior managers are apt to be flattered if they are convinced the approach comes from someone who is capable of going a long way. The following ground rules apply:

(a) Target one or two executives as potential mentors

Talk to other people to discover their reputation within
the firm. Is this person going places? Is he interested in
developing other people? Is he known for his teamwork?
Will he have time for a mentoring relationship or has he
just been given a major project that will keep him out of the
country for six months a year? Build up as accurate a picture
as possible of each mentor candidate to establish who could
be of most help to you in your career.

(b) Make yourself visible

It is not who you know that counts, but who knows you.
You have to make more senior management aware of your
existence. You can: volunteer for high profile projects; copy
senior managers in on memoranda and reports (it can pay to
deliver them in person, on occasion); attend company social
gatherings, including the annual general meeting, if you can;
contribute to the company newspaper and to outside media;
circulate copies of published articles or speeches you give.

(c) Show you have ambition and want to improve your abilities

Establishing the seriousness of your ambition to advance is
essential. If the opportunity presents itself, get the senior
manager involved in recommending training or reading that
will help you expand your experience and knowledge.

(d) Ask the potential manager formally, in person, to be your mentor

Most executives will be flattered and respond positively to
an approach in person, either agreeing or making helpful
suggestions as to who else in the company would be more
suitable. In the latter case they will often make introductions
or recommendations on your behalf. Even if you simply
receive a blunt refusal, you have at least established your
credentials as an ambitious employee, willing to learn.

5 Boss-subordinate mentoring

Although this book has deliberately concentrated on mentoring between people outside the boss/subordinate role, some of the main characteristics of formal mentoring, in particular counselling, advising and tutoring should nonetheless be part of every manager's task. As we have seen earlier, the full rewards of mentoring come more easily when the relationship is separated from the petty problems of discipline. Boss/subordinate mentoring often also runs greater risks of creating resentment among employees who are not privileged to receive such preferential treatment. These feelings can be contained much more readily when the manager is an outsider. When a relationship which is resented is within the department it may be a recipe for demotivation, reduced productivity and absenteeism.

One solution is for the boss to mentor *all* his subordinates, without favouritism. Even there, however, there may be unexpected dangers, as the following case illustrates:

A senior manager in a British nationalized industry was responsible for recruiting a new computing department, through first selecting a small team which he would personally train. This team in its turn would recruit more employees and use the same training methods. One of the original team members describes the unease the rest of the company demonstrated about the new department:

> The team had to travel around together and so we tended to get on well together and developed strong relationships which still exist today. In a company where staff morale is generally low, we attracted not only considerable attention but also some envy, both from managers and our mentor's colleagues. All of us, including our own trainees, had great respect and loyalty for our mentor. In the end the powers above became uneasy with the amount of power and influence he seemed to have. They also did not like the close-knit nature of the department. The solution they devised was to rearrange the organization and break the team up. It was a very successful ploy.

On the other hand boss/subordinate mentoring should and does work. Even in the case above, it was the success, rather than the failure of the mentoring arrangement that led to the problems.

Some firms, such as Jewel Companies, combine both types of mentoring. Jewel's Corporate Sponsorship Programme is small and provides a formal mentor to a selected group of particularly promising managers. For all the employees, their boss is expected to be their mentor. Says a company spokesman, 'We work to reinforce in all supervisors that a part of their role is to make the people who report to them successful.'

It is a part of each manager's responsibility to help subordinates grow. That is, in part, the way each manager is evaluated. Those managers who are threatened by their subordinates' growth tend not to reach key positions within the business. Thus, with regard to the middle and more senior management levels, there are few managers who do not recognize it as important to both the business and their own careers to help their subordinates grow.

Another company which makes good use of boss/subordinate mentoring is Bell Laboratories in New Jersey, which takes in up to 1,500 newly graduated recruits each year. The young engineers are paired with older, more experienced employees, often sharing an office with them in the initial months, until they have learnt the ropes.

So what are the characteristics of boss/subordinate mentoring? At base, they are much the same as for more formal mentoring, with the following exceptions:

(a) the boss is much more clearly involved in the younger person's daily routine work, although he should assign project work that broadens the protégé's experience and ability

(b) the problems of offending immediate line management are replaced by problems of being seen to be equitable to all the protégé's peers

(c) the boss can more directly and overtly groom his protégés as a potential replacement for himself

(d) in spite of the fact that only one hierarchical level may separate them, both may have to work a great deal harder to establish the frank-speaking, unthreatening environment that characterizes successful mentoring relationship. To put it another way, there are often things you don't want to tell your immediate boss.

These factors apart, boss/subordinate mentoring can still be a rewarding experience for both people. Within the limits of his own experience, the boss can make the protégé 'company-wise', offer career advice and direct him towards appropriate training. He can also be influential in helping the protégé, who would benefit from formal mentoring, to find a suitable mentor at a higher level. Indeed, if he succeeds in making this a tripartite relationship, the benefits to his own career may also be considerable.

6 What makes a mentoring programme successful?

In individual company terms, the objectives and measurements discussed in chapter 6 should provide an adequate assessment of whether the programme has done the job it was designed for. More generally, however, the following checklist given by Professor Andrew Souerwine to a Sundridge Park conference provides a useful summary of the features of a successful mentoring programme.

Successful mentoring programmes:

(a) have top management support
(b) are part of a larger human resources/career development effort
(c) consist only of volunteer participants
(d) tend to be made up of relatively short phases
(e) select mentors and protégés carefully
(f) have 'structured flexibility'
(g) make everyone aware of the problems that may arise
(h) have an effective monitoring system
(i) start small and grow
(j) orient both mentors and protégés before the relationship begins.

Bibliography

ACES NEWSLETTER 'Mentoring and networking', December 1981

ALLEMAN E. *Measuring mentoring, a manual for the leadership development questionnaire*. Available from Leadership Development Consultants Inc. Mentor, Ohio

ALLEMAN E. *What's really true about mentoring?*. Leadership Development Consultants Inc. Mentor, Ohio, 1984

ALLEMAN E, COCHRAN J, DOVERSPIKE J, NEWMAN I. 'Enriching mentoring relationships'. *The Personnel and Guidance Journal*, February 1984

ATKINSON C *and others* 'Management development roles: coach, sponsor and the mentor'. *Personnel Journal*, November 1980

ATKINSON J. 'Manpower Strategies for Flexible Organisations', *Personnel Management*, August 1984

BOVA BM, AND PHILLIPS RR. 'The mentor relationship: A study of mentors and protégés in business and academia', ERIC 208 233 1981, p 14

BOWEN DD. 'On considering aspects of the mentoring process'. *Behaviour Today*, 13 (15), 1982

BOWEN DD. 'Were men meant to mentor women?', *Training and Development Journal*, February 1985

BRIDGES RD. 'Mentors open new careers and hobby vistas for youth'. *Phi Delta Kappan*, November 1980

BRITISH INSTITUTE OF MANAGEMENT, *Mentoring*, MINT series, February 1987

BUREAU OF BUSINESS PRACTICE, 'Being a mentor', *Management Letter* 304, February 1990

BURKE RJ. 'Mentors in organizations', *Group and Organization Studies*, September 1984

BUSHARDT SC. 'Picking the right person for your mentor', *S.A.M. Advanced Management Journal*, Summer 1982

CARTER HM. 'Making it in Academia; Gurus, can get you there?', Paper presented at the annual meeting of the American Educational Research Association, New York, March 1982

CLAWSON J. 'Mentoring in managerial careers'. In CB Derr (ed), *Work, family, and the career*. Praeger, 1980

CLAWSON JG. 'Is mentoring necessary?', *Training and Development Journal*, April 1985

CLUTTERBUCK D. 'How much does success depend on a helping hand from above?'. *International Management*, April 1982

COLLIN A. 'Notes on some Typologies of Management Development and the Role of the Mentor in the Process of Adaptation of the Individual to the Organisation', *Personnel Review*, Vol. 8, No. 1, 1979

COLLINS EGC. *ed* 'Everyone who makes it has a mentor': interviews with FJ Lunding, GL Clements, DS Perkins *Harvard Business Review*, July–August 1978

COLLINS NW. *Professional women and their mentors: A practical guide to mentoring for the woman who wants to get ahead*. Prentice-Hall, 1983

COOK MF. 'Is the mentor relationship primarily a male experience?' *Personnel Administrator*, November 1979

CRANDALL HB. 'Are mentors necessary for successful careers?', *Direct Marketing*, October 1981

DALTON GW, THOMPSON PH, AND PRICE RL. 'The four stages of professional careers: A new look at performance by professionals', *Organizational Dynamics*, Summer 1977

DARLING LA. 'Mentor types and life cycles', The *Journal of Nursing Administration*, November 1984

DAVIS RL, GARRISON PA. *Mentoring: In search of a taxonomy, Masters Thesis.* MIT Sloan School of Business, 1979

DEUTSCH C. Guidance Counselors. *TWA Ambassador*, September 1983

Employee Relations Human Resources Bulletin, 'How to bring mentor and protégé together – formally'. Waterford, Connecticut, March 1984

FITT LW, AND NEWTON DA, 'When the mentor is a man and the protégé a woman', *Harvard Business Review*, March–April 1981

'Formal mentors help junior staffers advance at firms and US agencies'. *Wall Street Journal*, November 1983

FREY BA, AND NOLLER RB. 'Mentoring: A legacy of success', *Journal of Creative Behaviour*, first quarter 1983

GEORGE P, KUMMEROW J. 'Mentoring for career women'. *Training/HRD*, February 1981

GRAY JD. 'The management readiness programme at Merrill Lynch'. *The Career Centre Bulletin*, Vol 4, No 1 1983

GRAY WA. 'Achieving employment equity and affirmative action through formalized mentoring', Conference Proceedings of the National Conference on Management in the Public Sector, Victoria, B.C., Canada, April 21–23 1986

HALATIN TJ. 'Why be a mentor?', *Supervisory Management*, 1981

HALATIN TJ, AND KNOTTS RE. 'Becoming a mentor: Are the risks worth the rewards?', *Supervisory Management*, February 1982

HALCOMB R. 'Mentors and the successful woman', *Across the Board*, February 1980

HODGSON P. 'Managers can be Taught but Leaders have to Learn', *Industrial and Commercial Training*, November–December 1987

HUNT DM, MICHAEL C. 'Mentorship: A career training and development tool'. *Academy of Management Review*, 1983

INDUSTRIAL RELATIONS SERVICES, 'Mentors and their Role in Developing Talent', in the Recruitment and Development supplement to *Industrial Relations Review and Report*, 462, April 1990

INDUSTRIAL RELATIONS SERVICES, 'Back to Basics: Mentoring', in the Recruitment and Development supplement to *Industrial Relations Review and Report*, 464, May 1990

INDUSTRIAL SOCIETY AND THE ITEM GROUP, *The Line Manager's Role in Developing Talent*, Industrial Society, 1990

JOHNSON M. 'Mentors – the key to development and growth'. *Training and Development Journal*, July 1980, Vol 34, No 7

KAYE B, FARREN C, AND GRAY JD. 'Mentoring: a boon to career development'. *Personnel*. American Management Association, November 1984

KIECHEL W. 'Wanted: Corporate leaders'. *Fortune*, May 1983

KIZILOS P. 'Take my mentor, please', *Training*, April 1990

KLAUSS R. *Mentors and seniors advisors for executive development*, Washington DC, United States Office of Personnel Management, 1981

KLOPF G. 'The case for mentors'. *Education Digest*, January 1982

KONDRASULR J. 'The coaching controversy revisited'. *Training and Development Journal*, February 1980, Vol 34, No 2

KRAM K. 'Phases of the mentor relationship'. *Academy of Management Journal*, Vol 26, No 4, 1983

KRAM K. *Mentoring processes at work: Developmental relationships in managerial careers*. Doctoral dissertation, Yale University, 1980

KRAM KE, 'Improving the mentoring process', *Training and Development Journal*, April 1985

KRAM K, AND ISABELLA LA. 'Much ado about mentors, not enough about peers', *Career Development Bulletin*, 1983

KRAM KE, AND ISABELLA LA. 'Mentoring alternatives: The role of peer relationships in career development', *Academy of Management Journal*, March 1985

KRAUS R. *Mentors and senior advisors for executive development.* US Office of Personnel Management, 1981

LEAN E. 'Cross-gender mentoring: downright upright and good for productivity'. *Training and Development Journal*, May 1983

LEVINSON D. *The Seasons of a Man's Life.* New York, Alfred Knopf, 1978

LEWIN WB. 'Mentoring: A concept for gaining management skills'. *The Magazine of Bank Administration*, 1979

Management Review Editorial, June 1984

MILNE A. 'Mentor relationships: a subject for research'. CEPEC, 1983

MISSIRIAN AK. *The corporate connection: why executive women need to reach the top.* Prentice-Hall, 1982

MUMFORD A. 'What's new in management development', *Personnel Management*, May 1985

NEJEDLO RJ AND POWELL JA. *Mentoring and networking annotated bibliography.* New England College, 1984

NOLLER RB. 'Mentoring: a renaissance of apprenticeship'. *Journal of Creative Behaviour*, Vol 16, 1982

PETERS TJ AND WATERMAN RH. *In search of excellence.* Harper & Row. New York, 1982

PHILLIPS LL. *Mentors and protégés: A study of the career development of women managers and executives in business and industry.* Doctoral dissertation, UCLA, 1977

PHILLIPS-JONES L. 'Establishing a formalized mentoring programme'. *Training and Development Journal*, February 1983

PHILLIPS-JONES L. *Mentors and protégés.* Arbor House, 1982

PRICE M. 'Corporate godfathers by appointment only'. *Industry Week*, 1981

QUERART M. *The role of the mentor in the career development of university faculty members and academic administrators.* University of Miami, 1981

OSHERSON S. *Holding on or letting go.* The Free Press, 1980

REICH MH. 'The mentor connection', *Personnel*, February 1986

ROCHE G. 'Much ado about mentors'. *Harvard Business Review*, January–February 1979

SHAPIRO E, HASELTINE F, ROWE M. 'Moving up: Role models, mentors and the patron system'. *Sloan Management Review*, 1978

SHEENY G. 'The mentor connection'. *New York Magazine*, 5 April 1976

SHELTON C. 'Mentoring programmes. Do they make a difference?' *The NABW Journal* July/August 1982

SHELTON C, CURRY J. 'Mentoring at Security Pacific'. *The NABW Journal* July/August 1982

SHORT, BRANT AND SEEGAR M. 'Mentoring and organizational communication: A review of the research', paper presented at the annual meeting of the Central States Speech Association, Chicago, April 12–14 1984; ERIC ED 245 282

THOMPSON J. 'Patrons, rabbis, mentors – whatever you call them, women need them too'. *MBA*, 10 (2) 1976

ZALEZNIK A. 'Managers and leaders: Are they different?'. *Harvard Business Review*. May–June 1977

ZEY MG. *The mentor connection.* Dow Jones Irwin, 1984